I'm Fine
with God...

It's Christians I Can't Stand

Bruce Bickel
Stan Jantz

HARVEST HOUSE PUBLISHERS

EUGENE, OREGON

Unless otherwise indicated, all Scripture quotations are taken from the *Holy Bible,* New Living Translation, copyright © 1996. Used by permission of Tyndale House Publishers, Inc., Wheaton, IL 60189 USA. All rights reserved.

Verses marked KJV are taken from the King James Version of the Bible.

Verses marked NIV are taken from the HOLY BIBLE, NEW INTERNATIONAL VERSION®. NIV®. Copyright © 1973, 1978, 1984 by the International Bible Society. Used by permission of Zondervan. All rights reserved.

Verses marked TLB are taken from *The Living Bible,* Copyright © 1971. Used by permission of Tyndale House Publishers, Inc., Wheaton, IL 60189 USA. All rights reserved.

Published in association with the Conversant Media Group, P.O. Box 3006, Redmond, WA 98007.

Bruce Bickel: Published in association with the literary agency of Mark Sweeney & Associates, 28540 Altessa Way, Ste. 201, Bonita Springs, FL 34135.

Stan Jantz: Published in association with the literary agancy of Mark Sweeney & Associates, 28540 Altessa Way, Ste. 201, Bonita Springs, FL 34135.

ConversantLife.com is a trademark of Conversant Media Group. Harvest House Publishers, Inc., is a licensee of the trademark ConversantLife.com.

Cover by Abris, Veneta, Oregon

Cover photo © En Tien Ou / iStockphoto

I'M FINE WITH GOD...IT'S CHRISTIANS I CAN'T STAND

Copyright © 2008 by Bruce Bickel and Stan Jantz
Published by Harvest House Publishers
Eugene, Oregon 97402
www.harvesthousepublishers.com

Library of Congress Cataloging-in-Publication Data
Bickel, Bruce, 1952-
I'm fine with God—it's Christians I can't stand / Bruce Bickel and Stan Jantz.
p. cm.
ISBN-13: 978-0-7369-2197-8
ISBN-10: 0-7369-2197-4
1. Interpersonal relations—Religious aspects—Christianity. I. Jantz, Stan, 1952- II. Title.
BV4597.52.B525 2008
277.3'083—dc22

2007041325

Printed in the United States of America

08 09 10 11 12 13 14 15 16 / VP-SK / 12 11 10 9 8 7 6 5 4

Bruce Bickel and Stan Jantz are part of a faith-based online community called ConversantLife.com. At this website, people engage their faith in entertainment, creative arts, science and technology, global concerns, and other culturally relevant topics. While you're reading this book, or after you have finished reading, go to www.conversantlife.com/brucebickel and www.conversantlife.com/stanjantz and use these icons to read and download additional material from Bruce and Stan that is related to the book:

 Resources: Download study guide materials for personal devotions or a small-group Bible study.

 Videos: Click on this icon for interviews with Bruce and Stan and video clips on various topics.

 Blogs: Read through Bruce's and Stan's blogs and articles and comment on them.

 Podcasts: Stream ConversantLife.com podcasts and audio clips from Bruce and Stan.

conversant **life** .com

engage your faith

Contents

Introduction

Every segment of society has its members of the lunatic fringe, but Christianity seems to have a disproportionately high percentage of them. This fact wouldn't present any problems if Christians kept a low profile. For example, we're sure the Amish have a few wackos in their midst, but they don't get up in your face with billboards that hint at your eternal destination, and they don't try to impose their moral criteria as a filter on the public airwaves. Of course, the Amish don't use electricity, and that contributes to their cultural obscurity. But at least their goofballs remain an Amish problem that isn't inflicted on the rest of us.

Unfortunately, many Evangelical Christians don't have the unassuming qualities of the Amish. They are bold and brash with their oddities. They seem intent on exposing and publicizing their own peculiarities. The most weird among them rise to public prominence. Shouldn't the natural tendency be for Christians to keep their most bizarre brethren (and sistern) locked in the church basement (or cistern)? We could only hope so. But no, they are free to roam in society, subjecting all of us to a veritable religious freak show. You're probably already familiar with the cast that we're talking about:

- The clown (literally) who sat in the end-zone seats at every Super Bowl. He was easy to spot. He wore the rainbow colored wig, and he held up a large "John 3:16" sign when the television camera set up for a field goal attempt. Did he really think that people would stop watching the game on TV so they could look up that Scripture in a Bible that is conveniently nearby on the buffet table between the Budweiser and the pork rinds?

- The televangelist who harangues his cable-network congregation with fund-raising solicitations, sounding as if the Almighty God of the universe is impotent to keep the network going unless Granny signs over her monthly social security check: "Jesus wants to save you, but He can't afford to do it for free!"

- The Christian plumber who advertises in the yellow pages with a big fish symbol displayed prominently in the ad. The sign of the fish was an effective secret symbol among Christians in the first century AD, when being identified as a Christian meant being used as lion bait in the Roman Coliseum. But 20 centuries later that fish symbol means this: "Hey, come to me for your plumbing repairs. I may do a lousy job cleaning your clogged pipes, and I might charge you more than the other guys, but at least you'll be reamed by a fellow Christian."

- "Faith healers" who can cure diseases and ailments that people don't even know they have. Is their supernatural power divinely bestowed on them only during the hours of their televised crusade? If they possess the power continually, why don't they spend a little time walking through the corridors of their local hospital (or curing their own comb-over)?

But It Gets Worse...Much Worse

Perhaps such Christian lunacy and hypocrisy would be tolerable if for no other reason than for its periodic comic relief, but unfortunately it doesn't stop there. Some Christians invite disdain upon themselves—and the God they claim to represent—with despicable behavior that contradicts any notion that God is love. The gun-toting, bomb-planting, Christian antiabortionists are prime examples. In the name of their God, who loves unborn children, they maim and murder physicians, nurses, and patients at health clinics where abortions are performed. There is no theological justification for this heinous conduct. If God abhors the killing of unborn babies, doesn't He also loathe the illegal assassination of these health-care workers? Are these so-called Christians blind and brain-dead to this tragic irony of their atrocities?

Some self-defensive Christians might say the preceding paragraph cites an extreme and unfair example; surely such antiabortionists are mentally unstable. Obviously so, but what about the many other instances in which prejudice and bigotry run rampant in the Christian community?

The world is forced to suffer through the hatred harbored by some Christians every October 6. On that date in 1998, a 22-year-old college student named Matthew Shephard was bludgeoned by two men and left hanging on a fence in the nearly freezing temperatures of Laramie, Wyoming. Eighteen hours later, passing motorists discovered Matthew's almost lifeless body. This was not the first time Matthew had been beaten because he was gay, but it was the last time. He died after being in critical condition for several days.

The four people arrested in connection with Matthew's murder did not claim to be Christians, but the people who picketed Matthew's funeral proudly proclaimed their Christian faith. To our way of thinking, the behavior of a Baptist minister and his congregation from Kansas revealed perhaps more premeditated hatred than the murderers had. The signs held by these so-called Christians along the route of the funeral procession did not protest the murder; instead, they protested Matthew's lifestyle. Their message to Matthew's grieving family was clear: "God Hates Fags!"

Members of this church reiterate their bigotry annually on the anniversary of Matthew's death as they post similar signs near his grave. And the church's website keeps a running count of the number of days "Matthew has been in hell," including a picture of Matthew with animated flames burning around his face. And if you have the proper computer plug-ins, you can hear "Matthew's voice" scream from hell that you should listen to the church's pastor as he warns against the evils of a homosexual lifestyle. Personally, we don't want to hear what this pastor says, and we're sure that God doesn't want to hear it either.

God Doesn't Want Anything to Do with This

Whether these Christians are kooks, charlatans, or bigots, God doesn't want anything to do with their attitude and behavior. They degrade His name. They give a false representation of His character. They distract others who are sincerely searching for spiritual truth—and that is the reason for this book.

We've read bumper stickers that tell us that "Christians aren't perfect, just forgiven." But Christians don't need to announce to the world that they aren't perfect; this comes as no surprise to anyone. The fact is painfully obvious to every person who *isn't* a Christian. But we're not so sure it is obvious to the Christians themselves (despite the sticker on their bumper to the contrary). Even if they aren't part of the murderous and bigoted extremists, too many Christians tend to be hypercritical, self-righteous, judgmental, and intolerant.

In the marketplace of ideas, God deserves a fair shot. Whether people believe in Him or not ought to be their free choice. But God shouldn't be handicapped with the baggage of harebrained followers who claim His name but do not accurately reflect His principles.

We aren't on a crusade. (It is more of a rant.) We heard no booming voice emanating from the heavens (in a tone reminiscent of James Earl Jones) telling us to write this book. We're just fed up with Christians who give God a bad name. Yes, we assume that God can take care of Himself, and He doesn't need us to come to His defense. But we also want to make sure that people on a spiritual quest don't avoid God simply because so many Christians are repulsive.

We Have Met the Enemy, and It Is Us

If it isn't already obvious, in the interest of full disclosure you should know that we are Christians. (Actually, the term du jour is "Christ follower." Apparently the name "Christian" has become so sullied that those who are one desire a new moniker.) We are not trying to hide this information. In fact, mentioning it now gives us an opportunity to shamelessly plug the more than 50 books we've written about God, the Bible, and living the Christian life.

Like many other Christians, our spiritual gifts seem to be criticizing and fault finding. So it is easy and natural (not to mention enjoyable) for us to poke fun at other Christians. Who better than two card-carrying Christians to write a book denouncing the offensive behavior of the weirdos in the community of believers? After all, Christians are like a family that has a few crazy relatives. No one knows the strange and destructive behavior of Uncle Norman better than his own family members. And even though they all share a common bloodline, those family members have an obligation to report that he might be a danger to society. Consider this book our report about the eccentrics and misfits in the Christian family.

Even though there are two of us, we wrote the chapters of this book in the first person singular ("I," not "we"). Those who question the mental competence of religious adherents might use this as proof that we Christians each have only half a brain, and therefore, it takes two of us to write a book. We prefer to think that both of us have a full cranium and that we share similar Christian upbringings and church experiences, so we can speak for each other as we take turns writing.

Though we can speak for each other, we realize we can't speak for all Christians. We know that many will agree with what we say because they are equally embarrassed by certain Christian behavior. We are also pretty sure that many Christians will object with our assessment; they will be offended by what we say, especially if we feature them in the book.

Finally, allow us to make three more points of clarification. First, we really don't harbor animosity for any Christians in particular (or people in general). Our criticism is directed at the dumb things Christians do, not who they are. We are convinced that Christians are for the most part well-intentioned, although a few of them are often misguided. That leads us to our second point of clarification: Our criticism is primarily directed at the behavior of Christianity's lunatic fringe. We are never ashamed of God, but Christianity's overzealous extremists often make us embarrassed to be dressed in the same uniform they are wearing. So, for the most part, references in the following chapters to Christians refer to those in the tribe who are standing on the wobbly edge of rationality.

Rightly or wrongly, we exclude ourselves from this group. And that last statement provides a convenient segue to our third and final point: We realize that we ourselves are frequently guilty of behavior and attitudes that must embarrass and grieve God. We are probably most critical of others who have our same failings. That's why we can so easily spot the flaws. So why are their actions the target of our derision? Because they somehow manage a public display of their faux pas. We, on the other hand, have succeeded in keeping most of our ungodly conduct private—unless this book counts as conduct unbecoming a Christian.

So, to our Christian brothers and sisters we say, let's learn to laugh at ourselves, and let's learn from what we're laughing at. To those outside our Christian family we say, much of your criticism against us is well-deserved. But don't blame God. He agrees with you.

Bruce Bickel
Stan Jantz

I'm Fine with God...

but I Can't Stand Christians Who Impose Their Morality on Others

Can we start with the premise that Christians are not held in high regard in society? According to my purely anecdotal research, Christians have managed to slide down the societal acceptability chart to a position that is slightly below telephone solicitors and personal injury lawyers. For each notch they move lower on the chart, Christians raise the respectability of some other annoying segment of society. So by contrast, they keep looking progressively worse.

I'm sure I won't get an argument over this assertion from those who identify themselves as existing outside the circle of Christianity. But it may surprise you to know that many Christians don't argue with this premise either.

I frequently have the opportunity to speak before Christian groups. The audiences usually range in size from 200 to 2000 people. As often as possible, I use these forums to conduct an informal survey. I don't have any formal polling methodology; I just ask this simple question: "What one word best describes the reputation Christians have in our society?" Here are the most frequent responses:

- judgmental
- hypocritical

- self-righteous (which is really two words, but I grant it an exception because of the hyphen)
- ignorant
- pushy
- dangerous
- irrelevant
- obnoxious

When I review the responses to my question with the members of the Christian audience, they almost universally agree that they have this reputation in our society. (Duh! Apparently Christians aren't as clueless as you might expect. Despite their flaws, at least they can manage to get a blinding glimpse of the obvious.) But here is what I continually find to be amazing: These Christian groups always agree that this unflattering reputation of their own constituency is deserved and accurate. They readily admit that their group is not being falsely accused.

Apparently a lot of extremist Christians somewhere have been working very hard to earn their unflattering reputation. Maybe the rest of us need to concede that as a group, Christians are now the most annoying segment of society. Tell them they've won. Maybe then they'll give it a rest.

Unfortunately, their annoyance is so multifaceted that it won't be easy for them to cease and desist. Even if we assume that they desire to improve their social standing, the one-word character descriptors only identify the symptoms that are painfully obvious. A much more sinister underlying cause of these symptoms remains. Treating the symptoms will require dealing with that cause, and the lunatic fringe of Christianity may not be willing to go there. Radical surgery would be necessary—more than amputation (because the ailment is too pervasive). More than a lobotomy (which simply may be a redundancy). We're talking about a drastic measure: removing Christians from their self-appointed role as society's morality police.

A Brief Historical Interlude

Christianity began about AD 33 in the area surrounding Jerusalem as people began reporting that Jesus Christ had been crucified and came back to life. As with most of the known world at that time, Jerusalem was subject to the rule of the Roman Empire. For political reasons, Caesar let the Jews rule themselves in a semiautonomous fashion (as long as they paid their taxes to Rome). At this early stage, the upstart Christians weren't a nuisance to the Roman government. But the Jewish religious authorities weren't keen on this ragtag group that was promoting Jesus as the come-and-gone Messiah.

The Jewish Pharisees, who were the archenemies of the Christians, were stellar rule keepers. That was their gig. They were the largest and most influential religious-political party at the time; they controlled the operation of the synagogues and had tremendous influence on the general populace. The term "Pharisee" literally means "the separated ones," and that was an accurate description. The Pharisees separated themselves from the masses due to their strict adherence to the myriad of rules and regulations affecting worship, commerce, and everyday life (derived not only from the written Torah but also from the more extensive supplementary material in the Jewish oral law). They were known to be excessively rigid and intolerant with respect to the smallest deviation from protocols specified in the fine print of their laws.

Jesus was very critical of the Pharisees. He condemned them for caring more about the rules than their relationship with God. They were quick to condemn anyone who digressed in the slightest way from the behavior they considered appropriate. Jesus chastised them for following the letter of the law but completely missing the heart of the law. In one of his rants against them, he called them "a brood of vipers." I don't know the Hebrew symbolism behind that reference, but it can't be flattering.

Presenting the Twenty-First-Century Pharisees

In time, "Pharisee" became a name for a self-righteous, hypocritical person who took pride in behaving in a very correct and proper way and who felt morally superior to people who followed more relaxed standards. Now, 20 centuries later, does this remind you of anyone? Tah-dah! That definition fits many contemporary Christians (or at least their lunatic fringe). They are the Pharisees of the twenty-first century.

Representatives of the Christian clan are the first and most vocal to rail against any moral standard that doesn't fit within their tight-knit context. As a result, Christians are famous for their denouncement of the big-gies: abortion, homosexuality, and heterosexual sex between adults who aren't married to each other.

But just like the Pharisees of the first century, certain outspoken Christians have a long list of supplementary, seemingly minor moral infractions that they consider to be major offenses:

- celebrating Halloween

- watching *The Simpsons* (because it sacrilegiously portrays Reverend Lovejoy as a pious doofus)

- looking at ads in the Abercrombie & Fitch catalogue

- saying "Happy Holidays" instead of "Merry Christmas"

- drinking beer (not only because of the alcohol but also because of the sexually suggestive advertising)

Nothing would be wrong with Christians holding these opinions if they could keep them to themselves. Our culture has no gripe against people adhering to different lifestyles. We have no trouble assimilating Tibetan monks, astrologers, and vegans into our culture. We have all sorts of ethnic and philosophical subsets in our society, and we give them wide latitude to believe whatever they choose. For the most part, the vegans get along with the carnivores; neither group despises the other or tries to assert moral dominance over the other. But that is not the case with many Christians, who want to impose their morality as a mandatory standard of behavior on everyone, especially those who subscribe to a different (purportedly lower) moral matrix.

> Most Evangelical Christians presumptuously assume that their morality is the only correct one and that all other behavioral standards or codes of conduct are consequently wrong, flawed, and immoral.

No wonder that Christians who gallop through our culture on this high horse come across as self-righteous. And in classic slapstick comedic style (but not nearly so funny), one of their leaders falls off that high horse and into the sewer of hypocrisy when...

- A televangelist who shouts the loudest against homosexuality is arrested in the restroom at a playground for exposing himself to young boys.

- A Christian leader who condemns the materialism and greed of American society is caught embezzling funds from his ministry.

- A pastor who preaches the company line of stringent morality and encourages his congregation to picket the strip clubs and movie theatres is photographed sitting in a hot-tub with a naked woman who is not his wife (and the only thing he is wearing is a silly grin).

Another Dimension of Hypocrisy...and on the Lord's Day!

It is easy to be critical of others if you don't have to deal with their problems.

The Pharisees in the first century had an easier time following their hundreds of picky rules and regulations because they didn't really have to work for a living. They just had to be religious. Leaving a sheep in a ditch on the Sabbath, when no labor was permitted, was easy for them. But the poor Jewish schlep who owned the flock had to break the Sabbath rules and yank the animal out of the ditch if he wanted to have his livestock available for sale the next morning.

For a long time, Christians were critical of others over issues that the Christians managed to avoid altogether. But little by little, Christians fell victim to the same struggles and temptations as the rest of the population. And what do you think happened? Those things that were once grievous sins when the Christians weren't involved suddenly became more acceptable to them when they encountered the problems in their own lives.

> It's bad enough that some Christians project such a morally superior attitude, but their offense is at its worst when they don't live up to the standards they are trying to impose on the rest of us.

This is where Christians enter a further dimension of hypocrisy. The first dimension is when they do things that they preach against. But a more insidious dimension of hypocrisy is revealed when a former "sin" is recategorized as something now acceptable because so many Christians are guilty of it.

As late as the 1960s, many communities still enforced "blue laws." These laws were designed to enforce moral standards, particularly the observance of Sunday as a day of worship. Under these prohibitions, commerce was restricted. Retail establishments were required to be closed on Sundays. The activity of many communities came to a screeching halt on Sunday mornings. It was not merely coincidental that this was the time that Christians considered to be the Lord's Day, when there should be no labor (and apparently no fun outside of church). Christians disapproved of anyone promoting an activity or event on Sunday morning. Non-Christian men who were mowing their lawns on Sunday morning endured critical stares from Christian families driving by on their way to church. On Saturdays, people could do whatever they wanted, but on Sunday, only the pagans played. Even the NFL games were scheduled to start after Sunday worship services were over. Anything that threatened to take people away from church on Sunday was an evil influence that had to be avoided at all costs. The piety of the Christians on this issue was premised on the Fourth Commandment: Observe the Sabbath and keep it holy. Anybody who would argue with or disobey one of the Big Ten was on spiritually shaky ground. (Christians overlooked the argument of the Seventh-day Adventists that the Sabbath was really Saturday. Seventh-day Adventists have always been in the minority, so their opinion didn't count.)

But beginning with the decade of the 1970s, a gradual moral shift began. As the Christian baby boomers begat more babies, and as Christian soccer moms started raising pint-sized soccer players, skipping church on Sunday morning was no longer a dastardly deed. If you wanted little Jensen playing soccer, it was going to happen on Sunday because that was the only day the games were played. And little Jensen couldn't go alone; his game had to be a family outing, so the entire family missed church. If churches wanted parishioners in the pews more often than when the soccer team had a bye week, the preacher had to stop making the parents feel so guilty for skipping church on game days. And to keep the coffers replenished, churches figured out an ingenious way to collect a weekly offering from those soccer families: Hold a worship service on Saturday night! It might not be church on the Lord's Day, but at least it is church on the Lord's Day Eve.

I have no complaint with the many churches that instituted informal Saturday evening services to accommodate those in their neighborhoods who would be intimated by the more formal Sunday morning services.

Such concessions should be applauded. My grievance is with the hypocrisy of many churches that now provide alternatives to Sunday worship that permit Christians to treat Sunday as an ordinary day. These churches act as if this contemporary service scheduling makes them culturally hip, but not too long ago they were condemning a casual approach to Sunday because they considered it so sacrilegious. I've read the Bible. I know these Christians believe that God is immutable and that he never changes. I know they believe that his Word is the same yesterday, today, and tomorrow. So how is it that goofing around on the Lord's Day was such a heinous sin when it was convenient for them to gather on Sundays, but now, when they have frequent scheduling conflicts on Sunday, God has changed his mind about the Fourth Commandment? If they've got it right now, then they should admit that they had it wrong before. And somebody owes a big apology to all of those men who were mowing their lawns on Sunday mornings back in the 1950s and 1960s. (And my mom should admit that my eternal destiny would not have been jeopardized if I had gone to Donny Weller's tenth birthday sleepover party even though I would have missed Sunday school the next morning.)

Divorcing Themselves from Credibility

Christians have sometimes been experts at taking a moral stance based on a theological position, only to change their morality when their theological interpretation changes. When that happens, they are quick to assert the correctness of the changed position; they just aren't good at apologizing for being so dogmatically wrong in the first place.

This is not misconduct of which only contemporary Christians are guilty. It goes way back in our doctrinal gene pool. The case of Galileo comes to mind, and he lived 400 years ago. A Christian himself, Galileo is perhaps most famous for his published observations in 1610 that the moon, Jupiter, and Venus orbited the sun. His scientific opinions were in contravention of the widely accepted belief that every part of the universe revolved around the earth. Apparently the Christians at the time liked to think of themselves as the center of the universe, so they subjected Galileo to the Inquisition. Literally. The Inquisition of the Catholic Church consistently ruled against him from 1616 to 1633, resulting in a gag order against Galileo that restrained him from publicizing his theories. But as everyone now knows, Galileo's theories were correct. The Catholic Church got around to publicly admitting their error and later issued an official apology—in 1992![1]

Astronomy isn't the only subject on which Christians have changed their position. Divorce has been given an extreme makeover in the last several decades. Not too long ago, the D word was taboo in Christian circles. Good Christians never got divorced, although they might know someone who was related to someone (second cousin, twice removed) who had a divorce in their family. After all, the Bible says that God hates divorce, so Christians often shamed and humiliated anyone whose marriage ended in divorce. Apparently, it wasn't bad enough that the person had to endure the emotional, financial, and psychological drain of the divorce; Christians added spiritual shame and guilt to the list. Using the Bible like a sledgehammer, Christians beat down divorcées. The failure to keep a marriage (even a miserable one) hanging together disqualified a divorced person from preaching, teaching Sunday school, or saying the prayer at the start of the church potluck dinner. And if all of that didn't dissuade the divorced person from attending the church, he or she was subjected to further indignity with adult Sunday school class names like Pairs & Spares. There was no ambiguity about the second-class status in the church when the divorced members were labeled as "spares."

The Bible is just as clear about God's hatred of lying and gossiping as it is about God's stance on divorce. But Christians didn't discriminate against gossips (probably because it was a taint that the majority of them shared). Divorced people constituted a much smaller minority, so they were easy targets. Christians with a marriage license still intact belittled the tragic moral failings of those who didn't love God enough to stay married. To the face of the divorcée, the Christians sympathized in a condescending manner; behind her back, they ruthlessly spread rumors about her. At the woman's Bible study group, they read the passages that condemn gossip, never imagining that their own sin was perhaps more egregious in God's eyes than the divorcée's termination of her marriage to an abusive husband.

Thankfully, Christians have eased up on their selective criticism of divorce. Is this shift mandated by God's change of opinion of the subject? Absolutely not. But statistics reveal that the incidence of divorce in Christian couples has now reached about 50 percent (and slightly higher than in the overall population according to some surveys). This means that half of the congregants in a Christian church will have a divorce on their résumé. Do you really expect that a pastor will pound on the pulpit in condemnation of divorce if it will offend the charitable inclinations of half of the congregation when the offering plate is passed down the pews? And how can a church in Southern California expect to put only non-divorced people on the church board if 80 percent of the congregation doesn't meet that criterion? And who will do the preaching if the pastor is disqualified from ministry because his wife couldn't take it anymore and filed for divorce? And are you surprised that some clergy who receive compensation and benefits of more than $1 million per year from their ministries refuse to step down from their position (and lifestyle) simply because their marriage fell to pieces?

The frequency of divorce in Christian marriages has forced all of Christianity to consider divorce in a new light. And this is a good thing. Realizing that no one is immune from heartrending marital discord and breakup, Christians are compelled to be a little more gracious and understanding about it. But where is the apology for the decades of singling out divorce as being a worse spiritual failing than pervasive gossip and pride? Who is going to step to the microphone and admit that Christians were wrong to highlight divorce only because they weren't as frequently guilty of it?

> We must publicly acknowledge that Christianity
> has no rightful claim to moral authority in our society
> when it discriminates against the sins that are uncom-
> mon among its members, only later to soften that
> stance when Christians are discovered to be heavily
> involved in the formerly despised behavior.

How Did This "Holier than Thou" Problem Get Started?

In the first half of the twentieth century, people looked to the morality of Christians as the standard for acceptable behavior. That doesn't mean that everyone wanted to be a Christian or even agreed conceptually with the biblical view of God and Jesus. They simply considered Christians as moral people, and they considered the Ten Commandments, the Sermon on the Mount, and the rest of the "love your neighbor as yourself" principles to be fairly good benchmarks for societal interaction. (So much so that in 1956, Congress enacted the law that made "In God We Trust" the official national motto for America.) Even though people might not have agreed with Christian theology, they recognized that Christlike behavior was moral, upright, and a pretty good thing.

Christians survived well in this setting. Why shouldn't they? Christians were considered fairly respectable simply because they were presumed to be paragons of culturally acceptable behavior: They didn't smoke, drink, or cuss; they went to church; and they were supposedly honest, hard-working members of the community. Everything about the respectability of Christians was based on the prescribed behavior of their faith. Our society almost universally agreed that the Christian code of conduct was good, right, and true.

Over time, Christianity became defined more by its behavioral code than by its doctrinal beliefs. In other words, Christianity became a religion of do's and don'ts rather than a theological faith. This is exactly what Christ preached against when He butted heads with the

Pharisees. For him, the kingdom of God was all about relationship and the condition of a person's heart. He abhorred the thought that the kingdom of God would be minimized to rules and regulations and a behavioral checklist.

Notwithstanding what Jesus would think of it, Christians didn't seem to mind a checklist religion. They thrived on it. Admittedly, a checklist gives us an objective standard. We can easily determine how well we are doing (and we can just as easily determine how poorly someone else is doing in comparison). Jesus' approach of examining our own heart was way too subjective and ethereal. Without a checklist, Christians would have to independently think about whether their behavior was appropriate. A thorough analysis of propriety would involve the examination of motives and attitudes behind the actions. That approach was far too personal and involved too much soul-searching. It was so much easier to simply chant, "Christian men don't smoke and chew, and they don't date the girls who do."

A Reminiscent Walk down Legalism Lane

I was raised in one of those legalistic Christian households. Along with my sisters, I knew exactly what was expected of me (because my parents posted it on the refrigerator). I was born into the religious heritage of the Plymouth Brethren, which on the morality scale was slightly more conservative than the Pilgrims. Here is a brief glimpse of my Christianized life as an adolescent:

Playing cards were prohibited in our house because people used those "toys of the devil" for gambling. Other card games were permissible, but not the kind of playing cards used by sinners. My mother was apparently worried that if we had a regular deck of playing cards in the house, I would grow up to be a professional gambler, and my sisters would wind up being blackjack dealers at a strip club in Las Vegas. This prohibition presented some obstacles during my adolescence, but I managed to become a pretty good poker player with our Go Fish cards.

Music on the radio was usually playing in the background in our house, but my parents told me that our radio only got one station. How fortunate that the lone frequency was a Christian radio station. While children in pagan homes listened to the Beatles and the Rolling Stones, I repeatedly heard the greatest hit of George Beverly Shea (his vibrato-laden rendition of "How Great Thou Art" recorded live at one of the Billy Graham Crusades). Contemporary Christian music was in its infancy, but it hadn't yet made it to Christian radio because those musicians had long hair and didn't wear the customary white shirts and ties at church. The depth of their spiritual commitment was therefore questionable.

We had wine and other alcohol in our house, but it was used only for cooking, never for drinking. It was in the cabinet above the refrigerator, out of my reach. I was never tempted to drink it. Even at a young age I was smart enough to realize that the momentary pleasure from a single swig was not worth spending an eternity in hell. We never had any beer in the house, but we came tantalizingly close when I was about eight years old. Dr. Pepper released a drink called Pomac, which was like sparkling ginger ale with a shot of apple cider. All I remember is that it formed a head of foam when poured into a glass, and it was only sold in liquor stores. I called it "near beer" once but incurred my mother's wrath for doing so. Everyone in my family loved Pomac, but we didn't have it very often. My parents were forced to drive to a neighboring city to buy it because they didn't want anyone from our own hometown to see them walking into a liquor store. (I couldn't make this stuff up.)

Of course we had no cigarettes in our home. Smoking was the first step on Satan's Slip 'n Slide. I wasn't going to go there. I once saw a picture of my dad when he was in the army (before he met my mom and became a Christian). The picture was fuzzy, but my dad was standing around with a bunch of other soldiers, and I think they were all smoking. My dad never talked much about his army years.

We couldn't go to movies. Nothing was wrong with Disney films; my parents readily admitted that. But if we went to the good movies, people might think that we also went to raunchy movies, like those risqué James Bond films with Sean Connery as 007. So we didn't go to movies at all.

I went to public school because homeschooling hadn't been invented yet. Our town had a private Christian school, but most of the students weren't Christian and went there only because they had been kicked out of public school.

I don't remember ever having the sex talk with my dad, but my parents did give me a book to read. (No pictures.) I had been going to Sunday school my entire life, so by my teenage years I clearly knew the dangers of premarital sex: It leads to dancing.

Don't get me wrong. I'm not complaining about my upbringing. It was strict and religiously legalistic, but we had a great time together as a family. My parents loved me, and I can't fault their efforts because they wanted to make sure that in the afterlife I was going to have a mansion next door to theirs in heaven. They trusted me, but they imposed all of those rules because they didn't trust Satan.

My parents actually scoffed at Christians or wannabe Christians whose theology was based on the faulty premise of "do good and be good so you can go to heaven." Our faith was based on a personal relationship with Jesus Christ. I always sensed a cognitive dissonance about this. We sure spent a lot of time being good and doing good, and avoiding being bad and doing bad—much more time than we spent enjoying God. We Christians clearly had an image to maintain, and how we behaved and appeared to others was an important part of our Christian calling.

I was in high school and college during the era of Woodstock, the Vietnam War, and the cultural revolution. During these years, American culture experienced a megashift to the philosophies of relativism and postmodernism. (I know this because my college professors told me so.) I was a part of that first American generation to question whether truth existed. For the first time, the general populace was taught that what is right for one person may not be right for someone else. Instead of Christianity being the default faith in our culture, the predominate philosophies became religious pluralism (all religions are valid, each has an element of truth, and it doesn't really matter which one you believe because they all get you to the same place in the end) and naturalism (there is no divine supernatural power at work in the universe, science is the full extent of what can be known, and our existence is merely the result of random and uncontrolled events).

> As the twentieth century morphed into the twenty-first, American culture shifted away from social pressure to adhere to Christian principles as the singular accepted standard.

With this change in our culture's philosophical context, Christians were no longer the model for behavior and conduct. In fact, there was no single model that everyone was expected to follow. No longer was there a set of universally acknowledged moral behaviors. But Christians weren't savvy to this cultural shift. They kept expecting everyone to do what they did and to believe what they believed. Their attitude and their insistence on the correctness of their beliefs was precisely the opposite of what society now considered to be good, right, and true. Christians were desperately trying to lead society with their behavior without realizing that the culture considered them narrow-minded and judgmental for trying to do so.

Within a matter of a few decades in my life, Christians went from being respected in the culture to being rejected by the culture. I was an eyewitness to this train wreck.

What Does God Think About All of This?

Christians have assumed the role of twenty-first-century Pharisees, which is ironic because the Pharisees were the only ones Jesus criticized for their behavior. As an itinerant preacher of sorts, Jesus had occasion to hang out with the street people of first-century Jerusalem and the other towns and villages in Judea and Galilee. The socially acceptable members of society did not look favorably upon the people in his network of friends and family: the homeless, coarse commercial fishermen, prostitutes, dishonest tax collectors, lepers, and the like. Jesus' comrades were far from flawless, but he never chastised them for their behavior. Remember, he was the guy who said, "Let him who is without sin cast the first stone" when he was asked to pass judgment on an adulteress who was hauled before him by the Pharisees. Was Jesus indifferent to immorality? No, but he didn't evaluate people on the basis of their rap sheet or their curriculum vitae. To him, every person, regardless of his or her moral mess-ups, was full of worth and value.

The only people who raised Christ's ire were the Pharisees. His complaint against them was that they had placed themselves in a position of moral authority over the people, but they refused to acknowledge that they were just as morally flawed as those they demeaned. The Pharisees' hypocrisy and spiritual arrogance ticked off Christ.

Christians who desire to follow Jesus' teachings should pay particular attention to how much he abhorred the behavior of the Pharisees. Then they should examine whether their own conduct and attitudes fit the Pharisaical pattern. If Christians doubt that their behavior is offensive to Jesus, they should examine his characterization of the Pharisees when he publicly castigated them in his famous "woe to you" speech (Matthew 23:13-36). See if you think his descriptions fit many contemporary Christians:

- "Hypocrites! For you are careful to tithe even the tiniest income from your herb gardens, but you ignore the important aspects of the law—justice, mercy, and faith."

- "Blind guides! You strain your water so you won't accidentally swallow a gnat [to retain your ceremonial cleanliness], but you swallow a camel!"

- "Hypocrites! For you are so careful to clean the outside of the cup and the dish, but inside you are filthy—full of greed and self-indulgence!"

- "Hypocrites! You are like whitewashed tombs—beautiful on the outside but filled on the inside with dead people's bones and all sorts of impurity. Outwardly you look like righteous people, but inwardly your hearts are filled with hypocrisy and lawlessness."

> Would Jesus express the same indignation at many contemporary Christians? Maybe he is saying those very same things to them right now. But if he is, we'll never know because they aren't admitting it.

The Salt and Light Defense

I'm a lawyer, so please excuse me if I anticipate the arguments that Christians will make if they read and object to my observations in this chapter. (However, I expect that the Christians who are most likely to disagree probably won't read this chapter.) I anticipate that some Christians will say that God directs them to be behavioral models for society. They most likely will quote these words from Matthew 5:13-15 and make these arguments:

- "You are the salt of the earth. But what good is salt if it has lost its flavor? Can you make it salty again? It will be thrown out and trampled underfoot as worthless." Most Christians interpret this verse to mean that God wants them to flavor the culture with a moral influence, that they shouldn't blend in and lose their distinction. Instead, they should be a seasoning that enriches the culture.

- "You are the light of the world—like a city on a hilltop that cannot be hidden." Like the bright lights emanating from a city on a hill at nighttime, Christians are instructed by this verse to be shining examples of God's love.

- "No one lights a lamp and then puts it under a basket! Instead, a lamp is placed on a stand, where it gives light to everyone in the house. In the same way, let your good deeds shine out for all to see, so that everyone will praise your heavenly Father." Christians hide the light of their witness for God if they go along with the crowd or let Satan darken it. They are challenged to let the light of their Christianity shine brightly.

I have no argument with these verses, but perhaps I'm reading them a little differently. People are attracted to salt and light by their own volition. Something is appealing about the taste of the salt or the brilliance of the light that makes people desire more. That's how God wants Christians to behave. He wants their lives (their behavior and attitudes) to be so attractive and engaging that people are drawn to Christians on their own initiative. Those verses do not advocate cramming a five-pound bag of salt pellets down someone's throat. And they don't suggest that unsuspecting non-Christians be figuratively blinded by a halogen searchlight stuck in front of their eyes or that their body cavities be illuminated by a flashlight. Instead, Christians should live a life that is distinguished by their light and flavor in society without inflicting force and aggression on others.

I like the way God designed it:

- People can choose to leave the salt shaker on the table. Maybe they prefer their food to be sodium-free. Christians need to learn to let others ask them to pass the shaker.

- People can choose to view a city on the mountain from a distance. They shouldn't be forced to go and visit it. Christians need to realize that their light may be enjoyed better at a distance. In fact, they might look the best when they are the farthest away.

- Most lights are controlled by a switch. If the glare from the switch becomes annoying, the light can be turned off. Some Christians need an off switch because they are already annoying.

2

I'm Fine with God...

but I Can't Stand Christians Who Are Paranoid

In the last chapter, we discussed Christians who think they should be the moral arbiters in society. This chapters focuses on the Christians who recognize that they've lost that battle, so they want to withdraw from society (and to take God with them) because everything in society is so dangerously evil.

Some Christians actually enjoy being disenfranchised from society because that gives them an excuse to avoid contact with the "non-Christian world." They see sacrilege in every pair of True Religion jeans, they interpret every Victoria's Secret ad to promote promiscuity, and they perceive a satanic conspiracy with the Beanie Babies. Consequently, they choose to live in a cloistered universe and intentionally arrange the details of their lives to avoid contact with all of the sinners of the world (which includes the entire non-Christian population).

- All of their friends are Christians (and most likely attend the same church).

- They homeschool their children. (Christian private school is an option, but some of the kids who attend those schools aren't *really* Christians and therefore are bad influences on the campus.)

- They only select a business out of the telephone directory if the ad displays the fish symbol. But we are not talking about the regular yellow pages. No, that compendium is banned from these Christian households because it contains ads for escort services (which is presumed to be a euphemism for prostitution). They only use the *Christian* yellow page directory, which promotes an incestuous form of commerce in which you only do business with your own kind.

- They listen to Christian-only radio stations because that is the only way they can guarantee family-safe lyrics, programming, and commercials. They wouldn't want their teenage boys to hear any commercials about female hygiene products.

- They have a television, but they only watch the religious cable shows with the men and women hosts who have a high-hair coiffure. ("The higher the hair, the closer to God.")

- They only read Christian magazines and books. Although the same items are available elsewhere, they make these purchases exclusively at Christian bookstores and websites. General market retail establishments and websites also sell smut, like *Cosmo, GQ,* and *People* magazines, and those evil pornography empires shouldn't be aided by Christian dollars.

- They used to have a bumper sticker on their car that read, "Caution: In the event of the rapture, the driver of this car will vanish." They had to remove it. Their kids were beginning to wonder why so many other drivers gave them the One Way sign using their middle finger.

- They prefer to live in a Christians-only residential community, but unfortunately such discrimination is illegal. So they are stuck living in houses with pagans on either side of them. But there is no law that requires these Christians to be nice to their neighbors (or to even know them).

Let's clarify one point: The tragedy is not that a Christian chooses to make friends or do business with another Christian. And Christian bookstores, for example, have a depth of inventory that isn't available at most general market stores. The fabric of our society is woven together with affiliations based on common experience and shared beliefs, whether between Christians, Muslims, or Green Bay Packer fans. Rather, my objection is that certain Christians will have meaningful contact with and receive information from only sources that pass a "born-again Christian" litmus test. Anything or anyone else is blocked from their sphere by a "Jesus shield" that they have erected around themselves.

An All-Christian World Would Be Perfect (and Free of Tattoos)

I wish I were kidding about all of this, but you know I'm not. On almost any day, the story of a Christian who is trying to achieve cultural seclusion can be found in a major news source. For example, an NBC affiliate in central California reported the following story as this chapter was being written.

> A little girl with an ear infection was refused treatment and denied medicine by a pediatrician because of a tattoo. Not on the little girl, but on her mother. Maybe it was the mother's fault. Maybe she should have known better than to seek help from this doctor because the handwriting was on the wall—literally. He had posted a sign in his office that said, "Appearance and behavior standards apply." Apparently the mother should have known that her tattoo was an offense to God—because the physician certainly knew it. He imposes a "no tattoos and body piercings" rule in his practice based on his Christian faith. The physician said that he was simply following his religious beliefs in order to provide a Christian atmosphere for his patients.

How very Christian of him. Is it reasonable that a God-fearing,

Bible-reading physician who took the Hippocratic oath (or is that "hypo-critic"?) would deprive a little girl of medicine she needs for an entire night until a compassionate heathen physician could be found the next morning? Well, apparently so according to this doctor's interpretation of God's Old Testament law, which Moses pronounced to the children of Israel in the wilderness about 3500 years ago: "Do not cut your bodies for the dead, and do not mark your skin with tattoos. I am the LORD" (Leviticus 19:28).

But if the physician is that devoted, he surely lives by the other verses in Leviticus, including the rule found only ten verses away: "Love your neighbor as yourself. I am the LORD" (Leviticus 19:18).

Because this physician is so insistent on a comfortable, biblically correct atmosphere for his patients, I fully expect that he does not wear a lab coat made of a cotton blend in their presence. After all, Moses also decreed this law of God: "Do not wear clothing woven from two different kinds of thread" (Leviticus 19:19).

Devils and Demons and Fiends, Oh My!

The paranoia of some Christians about the existent evil in the world has them seeing demons all around them. The Bible does speak of supernatural forces in a metaphysical dimension, but I just don't see any demonic symbolism in the Easter Bunny, Cupid, Frosty the Snowman, or any of the Muppets. (I am declining to comment on Tinkerbell because this would take us into the hotly contested issue of the sexual orientation of fairies.)

Leave it to Christians to sap all of the fun out of a sweet and innocent holiday. Take this little quiz to see if you know whether a celebratory event is good or bad from the perspective of Christianity's lunatic fringe:

- New Year's Eve—bad. It is just an excuse to get drunk. Besides, the New Year's Baby is running around in only a diaper. We can't have our moral sensitivities offended by upper frontal nudity.

- Easter—good and bad. Church services on Good Friday and Easter morning are good. But the afternoon Easter egg hunt is bad because it promotes the Easter Bunny—who is nothing more than the devil in disguise attempting to steal attention away from Jesus. But Christian kids can see their neighborhood friends enjoying the Easter egg hunt, and we don't want them to feel deprived. So an alternative is provided: the eggs are Christianized and not laid by the Easter Bunny. And instead of candy, the resurrection eggs must be filled with strips of paper with Bible verses printed on them.

- First day of summer—very bad. This is really known as summer solstice. In many cultures, it is a pagan celebration during which the sun is worshipped (probably with naked dancing). No sun worship should be allowed. Only Son worship is acceptable.

- Labor Day—good. It marks the conclusion of summer and the end of bikini season.

- Halloween—are you kidding? Terrible. Historically, it was known as All Hallows' Eve or All Saints' Day. In pagan traditions, it marks the one day of the year when spirits can make contact with the physical world. Little children dressed up as ballerinas and firemen who walk around the block collecting candy should be told that they are pawns of the devil. We need to tell these four-year-olds about the satanic symbolism of this night. We need to scare the hell out of them. Literally.

- Thanksgiving—good. Anything started by the puritanical Pilgrims is a good thing.

- Christmas—good and bad. Advent is good. Increased church attendance is good. Baby Jesus is good. Nearly everything else is bad.

Again, I'm not making this stuff up. These are actual opinions held by some Christians about the evils of the world in which they are forced to live. These are their passionately held rationales for barricading themselves in the church. Lest you think I'm kidding, here is the text of an e-mail I received when I mentioned in an online bulletin board that I was writing a book about how much I was bothered by Christians:

> I couldn't agree more with you. Let me tell you my story. My sister-in-law and I used to be close friends. She got interested in spirituality, and talking with her sparked my interest. As I studied many different approaches, including the Bible and other religions, I began to understand that we are spiritual beings. My sister-in-law encountered a group of born-again Christians and abandoned her studies in spirituality. I was saddened that she had narrowed her beliefs so drastically, but I did not try to change her mind. We are still friends, but only distantly because her new tenets made her condemn my beliefs. Mostly our relationship soured because she offended me greatly when she called me the devil's pawn for being unrepentant that I had allowed my children to go trick-or-treating on Halloween.

> The paranoia of many Christians has caused them to circle their wagons. They are so afraid of imaginary evils that they keep their eyes closed and miss the good that is happening in society without them (and sometimes despite them).

Them Versus Us

Marketing specialists Jim Taylor and Watts Wacker have postulated several distinct "media communes" in the American culture. They researched magazine-buying preferences of American adults, and based on their data, they identified and labeled groups like these:

- sisters (women's shared interests),

- guys (sports and cars),

- intelligentsia (science and technology), and

- armchair adventurers (travel and recreation).

According to Taylor and Wacker, the most recent media commune to have come into existence is the one they call "God Talk."[1] This group is comprised of Christians whose dialogue is centered strictly around issues of faith. The characteristics of other groups were similar in many respects except for the subject matter of their magazines of choice, but the Christian group had two remarkably revealing distinctions:

- This group of Christians is the most tightly bound of all media communes. In other words, members of the other groups read magazines outside of their own category, but Christians do not.

- The Christian group is most defined by an "us versus them" mentality.

Many Christians' paranoia has caused them to remove themselves from society. In a scramble to shelter themselves from the cultural aspects they fear, they have removed themselves from any significant role in society and thus become irrelevant to it.

> Christians cannot expect to speak with any authority in the culture when they have marginalized and compartmentalized their own position in society.

Their fear has resulted in their cultural compartmentalization. It has become a self-fulfilling prophecy. They were afraid that cultural influences were going to overtake their beliefs, so they withdrew. But because they withdrew, they became known more as a demographic than for the doctrines of their belief. Their doctrines have gotten lost in the shuffle—not because society was opposed to the beliefs but because as a group they appear to have no cultural relevance.

In the Absence of an Enemy, Attack Each Other

Though these believers are living inside a cocoon, don't think they have lost their fighting spirit. They can be as hostile as ever, but now much of their fighting is directed at each other. The Christian army seems to be the only army in the world whose soldiers shoot at each other—on purpose. Their battles rage over issues that are monumental to them, but the rest of the world hears these arguments and laughs over the apparent triviality of it all:

- Were the six days of creation actual 24-hour days or longer periods of time?

- Charismatics are too emotional and don't have enough substance to their faith, and they shouldn't be allowed to have cable TV shows.

- Fundamentalists are so focused on doctrine that they are spiritually lifeless and impotent, and these snoozers shouldn't be allowed to have cable TV shows.

- Should baptizing be accomplished by body dunking or head sprinkling?

- The entire emergent church movement is out of control because young upstarts are beginning to question some tenets of the Christian faith.

- Should the liquid served at Communion be wine or grape juice?

- We aren't finished arguing about whether a woman can be ordained, and now we have to factor in the complication that the woman might be a lesbian.

- Should the choir wear robes or street clothes?

- Church music is too traditional and depressing; those old-fashioned hymns have to go. (And what does it mean when we sing, "Here I raise my Ebenezer"?)

- Church music has become too influenced by the devil music of the culture. Get the drums and electric guitars off the platform, and let's get back to worshipping God the way the Lord intended it—with a pipe organ and singing out of a hymnal.

As the publicity and notoriety of these Christian family feuds rise, any remnant of respect or credibility these Christians might have had is lost. The general populace takes these disputes as further and final confirmation that plenty of Christians are out of touch with the real world.

> Christianity is like a pregnant woman carrying septuplets. Those unborn infants are not fighting against the forces in the outside world. They are battling each other for survival and dominance within the womb.

Popping Their Heads out of the Sand

We might be inclined to pity these compartmentalized and culturally irrelevant Christians. They have been hiding for so long that they have lost all credibility to speak persuasively about cultural issues. Simply put, they have lost any influence they used to have. They are frustrated with this new reality, and their feelings usually intensify their resolve to step further away from the social debate and the marketplace of ideas.

But occasionally, representatives of the paranoiac Christians will pop their heads out of the hiding place to take a few verbal potshots at the culture. They don't stay around long because they just speak what's on their mind, and then they vamoose back into their protective womb. These drive-by rants usually have nothing to do with the current cultural conversation. Instead, they harp on any one of a few of their time-worn causes célèbres:

- attacking those who deny the existence of God,
- defending prayer in public schools,
- opposing the expansion of homosexual rights (now articulated in the form of opposition to same-sex marriage),
- opposing abortion, and
- fighting for family values.

Because these cloistered Christians haven't been active on the front line of social debate, they don't usually make a very good impression when they try to engage non-Christians in a battle of wits. In fact, they usually come across as desperate and mean-spirited. Instead of presenting a coherent argument on the merits of an issue, they simply invoke God's wrath and judgment on their opponent. At least that is how it seemed to author Sam Harris when he deflected the slings and arrows Christians threw at him following the release of his book *The End of Faith: Religion, Terror, and the Future of Reason* (in which he explains why he doesn't believe in God and why he considers people of faith to be a danger in modern life). The rebuttal from Christians who popped out of their hiding places was so vitriolic that it prompted Harris to write a second book, *Letter to a Christian Nation*. Here is the first paragraph from the preface of that second book:

> Since the publication of my first book, *The End of Faith*, thousands of people have written to tell me that I am wrong not to believe in God. The most hostile of these communications have come from Christians. This is ironic, as Christians generally imagine that no faith imparts the virtues of love and forgiveness more effectively than their own. The truth is that many who claim to be transformed by Christ's love are deeply, even murderously, intolerant of criticism. While we may want to ascribe this to human nature, it is clear that such hatred draws considerable support from the Bible. How do I know

this? The most disturbed of my correspondents always cite chapter and verse.[2]

Do Christians really think that they help their cause by entering unarmed into a battle of wits with a guy like Harris?

And Christians don't come across any better when they wave the battle flags on any of the other social issues they are notorious for fighting over. They come out shouting, but the rest of society nonchalantly rolls their eyes. They've heard the arguments before. And the rationale advocated by the Christians is always the same: "The Bible says..." to which many people resoundingly reply, "But we don't consider the Bible to be authoritative." As Christians keep pounding on the Bible as the supreme authority, they seem oblivious to the fact that their opponents don't feel any compulsion to read it, much less obey it.

Christians would scoff at the notion that they themselves would change their position on any issue if the opposition quoted chapters from a Dr. Seuss book. But, conversely, they can't seem to grasp that their Bible has no more persuasive authority with their opposition than that old Seuss favorite, *Horton Hears a Who!*

Whether the Christian arguments have any validity doesn't matter. The fact remains that their protestations are not being heard. No one is listening. Contemporary society views most Christians as unaware and ill-informed outsiders who are so removed from the culture that they are out of touch with it.

> Some Christians have removed themselves from the culture for so long that they are incapable of entering back into the cultural debates. They communicate as effectively as an armless mime.

When some Christians become painfully aware that they are losing the battle on a social issue, they bring out their "last ditch effort" bag of tricks. There are only two tricks in the bag—boycott and protest—and neither one is very effective.

Christian boycotts aren't working any longer because they can't generate any critical mass. For example, consider a Christian group's announced boycott of Disney over the company's decision to extend dependent medical insurance coverage to employees in same-sex unions. (You'll have to momentarily overlook the irony of criticizing Disney for its antifamily values when it is the world's leading provider of family entertainment.) If the boycott happened, Disney didn't notice. The Christian group had a constituency large enough to make a noticeable financial impact on Disney, but apparently most of those members were as crazy about Disney as the Animaniacs and exhibited more loyalty to the Magic Kingdom than to their denominational kingdom.

When boycotts aren't effective, Christian extremists often turn to protests (complete with placards held by marching children for that added family-values effect). Marching protests worked centuries ago, like when Joshua and his army of Israelites paraded around the walled city of Jericho. But more recently, protests have been ineffective. Have you ever heard of any people who changed their mind about the morality of abortion because they read a placard when they drove past a group of Christians protesting in front of an abortion clinic? Me neither.

Christians' continued use of boycotts and protests doesn't change anyone's opinion on moral issues. It just reinforces their opinion that these Christians represent a desperate and radical fringe group that isn't living in the real world.

Is It Paranoia If You Are Really in Danger?

Christians are afraid, and they have good reason to be. Various surveys give Christians plenty of reasons to worry.

- Seventy-five percent of Christian kids become disconnected with their faith when they go away to college.

- Church attenders are a shrinking percentage of the overall population.

- Many of those who identify themselves as Christians have doubts about the reality of Christianity.

Data like these give Christians plenty to pray about. But nothing indicates that contact with the culture is the culprit. These cracks in the foundations of Christianity probably were not caused because a couple of Christians used a plumber who didn't have the fish symbol on his truck or because they listened to a secular radio station instead of the programming on KGOD FM.

On this issue, Christians are being far too modest. I submit that loss in the ranks of the Christian army is the fault of the Christians themselves. They are scaring off their own.

What Does God Think About All of This?

Like a coach giving his team a pep talk before the big game, Jesus gave an impassioned speech to his disciples at the Last Supper on the night before he was crucified. It's called the Upper Room Discourse, but it could more appropriately be called the Everything You'll Need to Know When I Am Gone lecture. And then, like a coach who leads his team in a prayer before the game starts, Jesus prayed for his guys just moments before his arrest, which began the quick chain of events that led to his crucifixion. The Bible recites what Jesus prayed, and it includes this request that Jesus made to his heavenly Father regarding the disciples: "I'm not asking you to take them out of the world, but to keep them safe from the evil one" (John 17:15).

Just five verses later, as Jesus continued his prayer, he made it clear that his prayer was intended not only for his disciples but also for all Christians who would come after them: "I am praying not only for these disciples but also for all who will ever believe in me through their message" (John 17:20).

These verses are well-known to most Christians today, who use them to explain that they consider themselves to be only visitors on earth because their citizenship is in heaven. They refer to John 17:15 for the proposition that God wants them *in* the world, but not *of* the world. So they sing songs that bemoan their earthly existence while waiting for the angels to beckon them to heaven's open door.

In but Not Of

Christians who hide from the culture misapply this "in but not of the world" verse. They use it incorrectly as a rationale for their paranoia. They say, "Sure, we are forced to be living in the world until God calls us to our eternal home in heaven, but until that glorious event happens, we are supposed to avoid the evil influences of society so we do not become *a part of* the world." This interpretation misses the point and promotes a false doctrine of separation.

If God truly wanted Christians isolated from society, he could have easily designed that feature into his grand divine plan. He could have arranged for them to be sucked up to heaven immediately upon their conversion.

> Step 1: Say the sinner's prayer and ask Jesus into your heart.

> Step 2: Kiss your troubles goodbye because in a twinkling of an eye you'll be standing in line at the pearly gates.

But God didn't plan it that way. The biblical evidence is clear that God intentionally wants his Christians left in the world. Remember what Jesus prayed to his heavenly Father: "I'm *not* asking you to take them out of the world." Furthermore, he didn't expect his disciples to hide in some holy hole when he was gone or to barricade themselves in a monastery where they would be insulated from contact with the pagan world. His prayer for the disciples (and for Christians to follow) proves that he had in mind that they would be mixing it up with the members of society in the same way he had been doing for the three years of his public ministry: "As you [God] sent me [Jesus] into the world, I am sending them [the disciples and all other Christians] into the world" (John 17:18).

If Jesus wants Christians to go into the world just as he went into the world, then he wants Christians to be hanging out with sinners, the homeless, and the outcasts of society. He wants them befriending the prostitutes, the tax cheaters, and the good ol' boys. But he doesn't want them pretending to be religious and segregating themselves from the general public (which was his criticism of the Pharisees).

> Of course God wants Christians to be visible in society instead of hidden from it. If they are supposed to be salt and light in the culture, they have to be visible.

Transformation, Not Relocation

Christians make a huge mistake when they think God wants them to be segregated from society and huddled in their own holy communes. Salvation is not about being relocated away from society; it is about being spiritually transformed on the inside.

When people are saved by belief in Jesus Christ as their personal Savior, they don't change their geographic location. As they close their eyes and say a prayer for salvation,

- they are not immediately transported to heaven,

- they do not black out and wake up from their spiritual stupor in a mansion or cathedral,

- they aren't cosmically transported to the Vatican, and

- they don't open their eyes from the prayer and find themselves sitting on the stage at a Billy Graham Crusade or in the guest chair on a religious cable talk show.

No, wherever they were when they started their prayer is where they are when it is over. (This is true even for people in Winnemucca, Nevada who pray, "God, I'll accept you as my Savior if you take me out of this place." God will do the saving part, but he won't do the transporting part. They'll still be in Winnemucca.) And their circumstances are the same: same family, same job, same debts, same problems. Salvation is not about relocation.

But it *is* about transformation. Here is how the apostle Paul describes the transformation process of Christianity:

> And so, dear brothers and sisters, I plead with you to give your bodies to God because of all he has done for you. Let them be a living and holy sacrifice—the kind he will find acceptable. This is truly the way to worship him. Don't copy the behavior and customs of this world, but let God transform you into a new person by changing the way you think. Then you will learn to know God's will for you, which is good and pleasing and perfect (Romans 12:1-2).

God's plan for Christians is not to take them out of the world. Instead, he wants to transform them into a new kind of person who has his characteristics instead of their flawed ones. Of course, he doesn't want them copying the immoral behavior and conduct of the world, but living *in* the world (and coming into contact with non-Christians) won't be a problem if they have truly transformed their outlook to conform to God's principles.

When Christians transform their thinking to be in alignment with God's principles,

- they understand God's big picture,

- they don't get sucked into the world's mentality, and

- their behavior will be prompted by God's principles and not by peer pressure to conform to the worldly influences around them.

Instead of removing Christians from their problems and circumstances, salvation gives them a spiritual perspective so they can deal with those situations. And if Christians get with God's program, they won't have to be so paranoid about the world's influences. By staying tuned to God's wavelength, Christians should be able to handle exposure to a non-Christian environment without an irrational fear of being infected by it.

I'm Fine with God...

but I Can't Stand Christians Who Think They Are Correctly Right and Everyone Else Is Wrongly Left

A lot of people are mad at God these days, but really they're mad at people who claim to be speaking for God or at the very least call themselves God-fearing. Nowhere does this anger vent itself more openly and colorfully than it does in the political arena, where more than a few God-fearers have flexed their spiritual muscle in the past few years. Politics is enough of a hot-button topic without bringing religion into the mix (the analogy of pouring gasoline on a fire comes to mind). But when spiritual leaders with millions of followers declare war on the culture and do all they can to influence Washington lawmakers to vote their way—make that God's way—the fur really can fly.

People used to follow an unwritten rule about never talking about politics and religion in the same conversation. That's because sensible people knew that such discussions inevitably erupted into arguments, thereby ruining otherwise perfectly good friendships and family relationships. When I was growing up, we had some relatives nearby who did not share our family's political persuasions. I wasn't old enough to vote, and my level of understanding of the critical political issues of the day was rudimentary at best. But that didn't stop me from adopting my dad's conservative position without question.

Adopting a political position was a bit easier in the black-and-white

1960s, the decade of my adolescence. The specter of Communism hung over the free world like a dark cloud, so conservatives naturally rallied against the "red menace," represented most passionately by the Soviet Union and its colorful leader, Nikita Khrushchev. Let me tell you, when that nasty-looking Communist leader (at least he was nasty-looking to me) allegedly smacked his shoe on the podium and snarled, "We will bury you," I was ready to go out and fight the Commies all by myself.

My dad, who was as conservative and flag-waving as they came, used to sit me down at our dining room table and play recordings of political commentators like Phyllis Schlafly (a 1960s hair-up-in-a-bun version of Mary Matalin) on his reel-to-reel Wollensak tape recorder. I didn't really care for these sessions, which would be punctuated by my father voicing enthusiastic agreement, but I listened and was sufficiently indoctrinated to be able to hold my own in an informal debate, which didn't happen all that often because, as I said earlier, people didn't discuss politics or religion all that much.

Which brings me back to my relatives. My family didn't knowingly associate with liberal-minded folks. In fact, I don't think we even knew any liberals except our relatives, which makes sense since our family associated only with like-minded churchgoing conservatives. And the only reason we got together with our relatives was because they were, well, family.

In reality, our relationship went way beyond the blood ties. It wasn't like we got together on rare occasions because we had an obliga-tion. We really liked this family. My dad enjoyed their company and often talked about them in glowing terms unless the subject turned to politics and he was able to reference a view they may or may not have had. Since the subjects of politics and religion were taboo when we got together, I don't know if my dad ever knew exactly what they believed politically except that they voted for Hubert Humphrey in the 1968 presidential election, a fact that slipped out over dinner one night.

Nothing else was said. No argument ensued. It was just a something that came out, almost incidentally.

I say all of this to reinforce the notion that keeping politics and religion out of certain conversations was a good idea then, and it's probably a good idea now, especially if we are to remain on speaking terms with friends and relatives and, on occasion, perfect strangers. Even more, it's a good idea because the volatile mix of politics and religion can easily create a vapor cloud that may keep someone from getting closer to God.

That's not to say that politics and religion never belong in the same conversation. In fact, to keep them out of the public discourse is to deny the expression of two of the most basic qualities found in the human experience—law and faith. If law is the tangible moral code we collectively write and observe in order to function together in a material world, then faith is the intangible spiritual code written on our hearts in order to connect us and our material world to a heavenly world. Many people believe they both come from God. If that's the case (and I think it is), then we should be able to talk about them in ways that help us get a better handle on our world, our culture, and the way we interact with both in ways that are helpful and healthy.

But I digress. Before getting into the "I'm Fine with God" part of this chapter, I need to reflect on what happens when religion and politics mix in a most unhelpful and unhealthy way, and why I can't stand Christians who think they are correctly right and everyone else is wrongly left.

> If law is the tangible moral code we collectively write and observe in order to function together in a material world, then faith is the intangible spiritual code written on our hearts in order to connect us and our material world to a heavenly world.

Red and Blue

We are all familiar with the whole "red state, blue state" descriptions
of conservatives and liberals, Republicans and Democrats, and the
religious right and progressive left who supposedly live side-by-side
in this country. You've seen the maps showing a nation divided: The
blue states are on the coasts and the red states (designated by some
as the "flyover" states) are in the vast middle. The blue states include
the capitals of media and art, and the red states cover the American
heartland.

I took a while to get used to the idea that my heritage and ideologies
clearly put me in the middle of the red states (even though I live in the
blue state of California). That just seemed so bizarre for someone raised
in a world where the only true enemy was Communism. Why couldn't
I be a blue-state guy? Blue is my favorite color. It's a cool, soothing,
agreeable color. Red is hot and volatile. Red wants to take over.

As I think about it now, especially in light of the deep divisions that
have developed between red states and blue states, I'm not so sure
that designation, which we have all gotten used to, is all that helpful.
In fact, it might even be destructive. The outspoken pundits on both
sides rarely promote helpful and healthy dialogues and beneficial
debates, whether in the political or the religious arena. It's all yelling
and finger pointing with accusations flying. It's all about being right,
which means the other side is clearly wrong. Meeting together in a
kind of demilitarized middle zone, where people can love and respect
one another while holding opposing opinions, is rare.

We used to meet our relatives in such a zone. We not only kept the
relationship going, we even deepened it because we loved and
respected one another. This is the zone where Yankee fans and Red
Sox fans used to meet after the game. This is the zone where Ronald
Reagan and Tip O'Neill used to meet for cocktails after the political
business of the day was finished. This zone, this middle ground, has
all but disappeared in our culture. Yankee fans hate Red Sox fans and

vice versa. A conservative politician wouldn't be caught dead with a liberal politician (at least not in public). The border between red and blue is a thick black line, and to step over it is to step into the enemy's camp.

We Started It

Whenever a fight erupts—and clearly the red state people are fighting with the blue state people—onlookers naturally want to know who started it. In the current so-called culture war, that's not so easy to determine. Finding a ground zero for the culture war is difficult if not impossible. Even if one side did come up with a time and a place when the other side started the hostilities, the other side would disagree and start another battle.

That's why I'm going to go out on a very long limb and say something that may upset some people: I believe we red-state people started the current war between the states. Even more specifically, I'm referring to the members of the religious right, which includes a whole lot of Christians. We fired the first shots because we thought the other side was our enemy, or worse, the enemy of God and America.

Maybe the first shot was fired when the Moral Majority was formed in the late 1970s. Or maybe the fight began with a collection of shots volleyed by a variety of radio and television preachers and powerful pastors. It's hard to say. But the accumulation of the disgust expressed by these God-fearing leaders over the liberal leanings of certain politicians—not to mention the "moral filth" pouring out of the sin factory known as Hollywood—created an offensive strategy that fed upon the fears and took advantage of the good intentions of middle Americans. Emboldened by the political success of many conservative candidates who promoted family values, this previously silent majority became exceedingly vocal and increasingly powerful, known more for what it was against than what it was for.

I believe we red-state people started the current war between the states. Even more specifically, I'm referring to the members of the religious right, which includes a whole lot of Christians.

Red Is Righteous

For a politician to espouse family values is one thing. I'm all for it. The family is God's idea. We need to do all we can to protect and preserve it, and sometimes that means creating laws to do just that. I am convinced that red- and blue-state people can agree on this principle, although we may disagree on the methods. But when certain red-state people of great influence claim that they are speaking for God, they create problems. Mutual trust turns into suspicion, and disagreements become fights. After all, how do you argue with someone who claims to have a direct link with the Almighty, whether it is tethered to a vision or to a certain way of reading the Bible? A claim like that puts people who don't believe in God—and more than a few people who do—on the defensive, and before long, they push back.

Can you blame them? Whether they are correct in their perceptions or not, they believe the religious right is demolishing the wall separating church and state, and they fear that the God-fearers (who for the most part characterize the religious right) are making faith a condition of being a good American, not just a good Christian. Katha Pollitt, a progressive columnist for *The Nation*, speaks for many who perceive that the religious right not only has seized the moral high ground in the political process but also is shaping public policy.

> It's one thing to show respect for religious belief in the context of social tolerance in a pluralistic society—freedom of speech, separation of church and state, live and let live—but when Christians make faith a matter of public policy, it becomes hard to explain why nonbelievers should be deferential. If I wanted to live in a theocracy, I would move to Tehran.[1]

The New Atheists

Another one of my memories from the 1960s is the appearance on the cover of *Time* magazine of this startling headline: "God Is Dead." It wasn't a divine obituary as much as a report on the Death of God movement that came out of the thinking of some American theologians who believed that the culture had lost a concept of the transcendent God, not that God was literally dead. What they were intending to say didn't really matter because the name of their movement and the headline in *Time* were enough to send most people into an anti-atheist binge. Since the Death of God theologians were a bunch of stiffs who spent their time in academic ivory towers, the American public needed a visible target, and they found one in the mercurial and outspoken Madalyn Murray O'Hair, the founder of American Atheists.

For nearly four decades, atheists were like a scourge, and no one wanted to be associated with them. They existed on the fringes of society, especially as the religious right ascended to its place of power. Then, just a few years ago, something happened that turned the tide for those who believe that God is indeed dead, or rather, that he doesn't exist and never has. Atheism got popular.

This turnabout didn't happen in a vacuum. I believe that the atheists, or "nonbelievers" as we believers sometimes call them, were fed up with the pride and power of the religious right. Having been marginalized and labeled as "godless"—or worse, un-American—they decided to attack the head of what they perceived to be a budding theocracy— God. (For the record, God has never claimed to lead any one nation except for the nation of Israel, and that was thousands of years ago. Rather, people who claim to be speaking for God—through visions or direct revelation—have invoked his name and made him the head of a kingdom on earth that includes both church and state.)

So far the strategy for the atheists has been to write a series of books that have sold in much greater numbers than anyone on either side might have imagined. Led by Sam Harris (an American graduate student and the author of *The End of Faith*), Richard Dawkins (an Oxford professor and the author of *The God Delusion*), and Christopher Hitchens (a British-American journalist and the author of *God Is Not Great*), these "new atheists" have apparently awakened a new silent majority that includes millions of people (if book sales are any indicator).

Many philosophers and scholars contend that the arguments presented in these books are specious and surprisingly uninformed, lacking the kind of careful scholarship that has historically supported arguments for and against the existence of God. Nevertheless, the new atheists have the megaphone, and they are shouting louder than anyone else.

Some debates and a few conversations with the new athiests have included thoughtful Christian thinkers. For example, *Time* magazine invited Richard Dawkins and Francis Collins to engage in a dialogue that proved to be very fruitful. *Newsweek* set up a civil debate between Sam Harris and Rick Warren that revealed little more than the personalities of each man (Warren is larger than life, while Harris is quiet and reserved). At least the two were talking together in a mutually respectful manner. But these two examples may be the exception.

In some speeches and debates, the new atheists have resorted to name-calling. Both Dawkins and Hitchens routinely call anyone who believes in God an idiot. Should we be surprised? After all, haven't we Christians resorted to name-calling ourselves? Haven't believers been guilty of calling their unbelieving counterparts idiotic?

To me, the scandal is not so much that unbelievers are now bold enough to insult us believers. Let's accept the fact that they are sick and tired of being ignored and insulted themselves. No, the bigger scandal is that we are surprised by this rather sudden turn of events. Didn't Jesus tell us that the world would hate us, just as it hates him? And what ever happened to "turn the other cheek" and "love your enemies"? Evidently we don't take those words (also from Jesus) to heart. Rather than responding to our enemies with love and compassion, many of us in the heat of battle fall back on this old defense: "Well, at least we're not going to hell." Whether we merely think that or openly express it, finding comfort in that concept is both shameful and unbiblical.

The truth is that those of us who believe and have committed ourselves to the truth that God exists and has personally communicated to his human creation need to see this new development of aggressive, popular atheism as a good thing. God is in the conversation. The door is open to talk about him, not as a being who is interested in shaping public policy, but as someone who wants more than anything else to have a relationship with us, regardless of what we think of him.

> Rather than responding to our enemies with love and compassion, many of us in the heat of battle fall back on this old defense: "Well, at least we're not going to hell." Whether we merely think that or openly express it, finding comfort in that concept is both shameful and unbiblical.

What Does God Think About All of This?

God has given us a number of principles that touch on politics and religion, including the idea that the two should be separated. The Bible actually speaks directly to this issue through an encounter Jesus had with two groups—one religious and the other political. The story is told in Matthew 22:15-22.

In this famous exchange, some Pharisees—the group of religious legalists we met earlier—decided to confront Jesus in order to trap him into saying something that would get him into trouble with the state. The state, of course, was the Roman Empire, which was also the official religion of the day. Caesar was considered a deity as much as he was an emperor, and the citizens of Rome were expected to worship him accordingly. The Roman state tolerated the Jews and their religion as long as they paid their taxes and didn't make any trouble. Likewise, the Pharisees and the other Jewish religious groups tolerated Rome, although they hated the Romans and their occupation of Palestine. (The Zealots were the exception to this attitude of toleration. They advocated and initiated a number of failed armed revolts against Rome.)

The Pharisees also opposed Jesus, a revolutionary who was a huge thorn in their side mainly because he threatened their religious system with revolutionary ideas, such as loving your enemies rather than hating them. Consequently, they were always looking for a way to get Jesus into trouble. Usually they tried to trip up Jesus on some kind of religious technicality, but this tactic never worked because Jesus knew the religious laws—and especially the spirit of the law—much better than the Pharisees did. So this time they tried to entrap him on a civil matter.

As you read the passage, you can see that the Pharisees enlisted the support of some "supporters of Herod," who was the local ruler installed by Rome to keep the peace in Palestine. As you can only imagine, the Pharisees and the Herodians were bitter enemies. But in this case they put aside their differences and formed a strategic alliance against Jesus, hoping to get him arrested and out of their collective hair.

The Pharisees and Herodians decided to make taxes the issue. They came up with a question that had all the appearances of setting the perfect trap. If Jesus advocated paying taxes to Caesar (the state), the Pharisees would say he was opposed to God, making him an enemy of their religion. If Jesus said that taxes should not be paid, he would be considered an enemy of the state.

Now that you know the background, watch how the dramatic scene unfolds. The Pharisees and the Herodians speak first.

> "Teacher," they said, "we know how honest you are. You teach the way of God truthfully. You are impartial and don't play favorites. Now tell us what you think about this: Is it right to pay taxes to Caesar or not?"
>
> But Jesus knew their evil motives. "You hypocrites!" he said.

"Why are you trying to trap me? Here, show me the coin used
for the tax." When they handed him a Roman coin, he asked,
"Whose picture and title are stamped on it?"

"Caesar's," they replied.

"Well, then," he said, "give to Caesar what belongs to Caesar,
and give to God what belongs to God." His reply amazed
them, and they went away.

The way Jesus handled this is pure genius. He avoided the trap set
for him by showing that his followers have a dual citizenship. Our
citizenship in the earthly state requires that we pay for the benefits and
services we receive. Later, the apostle Paul would give this advice:

Everyone must submit to governing authorities. For all authority
comes from God, and those in positions of authority have
been placed there by God. So anyone who rebels against
authority is rebelling against what God has instituted, and
they will be punished. For the authorities do not strike fear
in people who are doing right, but in those who are doing
wrong. Would you like to live without fear of the authorities?
Do what is right, and they will honor you.

Pay your taxes, too, for these same reasons. For government
workers need to be paid. They are serving God in what they
do (Romans 13:1-3,6).

In addition to being citizens of earthly kingdoms, we are citizens of
God's spiritual kingdom, and that requires that we make God and his
work our first priority. That's what Jesus meant when he said, "Seek the
Kingdom of God above all else" (Matthew 6:33).

How does this dual citizenship play out in real life? Do people of
faith have a responsibility to influence the policies of their government,
or should they keep their noses out, as the new atheists would advocate?

Rebuild the Wall
slogan on Christopher Hitchens' website

As I've thought about this, I've come to the conclusion that in order for Christians to be in the world but not of the world—in order for us to engage the culture in a way that shows we love God and others—we need to remember two things.

Remember Who We Are

We've seen that the Pharisees were known for their self-righteous demeanor and hypocritical attitudes. They dripped with spiritual pride as they set themselves up as the moral authority for the culture, and Jesus called them on it. When we set ourselves up as the moral authority in our culture, we are acting just like the Pharisees. We relate to others much better when we remember that we are sinners saved by grace. That's not an excuse to sin but an acknowledgment of our sinful natures. The apostle Paul was well aware of this condition.

> And I know that nothing good lives in me, that is, in my sinful nature. I want to do what is right, but I can't. I want to do what is good, but I don't. I don't want to do what is wrong, but I do it anyway (Romans 7:18-20).

A Pharisee—either ancient or modern—would have a hard time admitting that, but you know what? We need to admit it. We're no better than any other person. The only difference between those of us who embrace the person and work of Christ and those who don't is that we have the power of Christ in us, and that gives us the potential to live a life that pleases God (Romans 7:24-25).

Jesus, of course, knows his followers intimately, and he knows that one of our natural tendencies is to judge other people because we think we are better than they are. Our judgmental attitude expresses itself in all kinds of ways but never more profoundly than in the way we judge those with a political viewpoint (or a personal lifestyle) that we think is offensive to God. When we do this, we are setting ourselves up as a self-righteous judge and jury, which really irritates people in the culture around us. It also irritated Jesus, who gave this stern advice to his followers:

> Do not judge others, and you will not be judged. For you will be treated as you treat others. The standard you use in judging is the standard by which you will be judged.
>
> And why worry about a speck in your friend's eye when you have a log in your own? How can you think of saying to your friend, "Let me help you get rid of that speck in your eye," when you can't see past the log in your own eye? Hypocrite! First get rid of the log in your own eye; then you will see well enough to deal with the speck in your friend's eye (Matthew 7:1-5).

Paul agreed, saying that when we judge others, we are in effect judging ourselves because we do the same thing we accuse them of doing (Romans 2:1). And by the way, Jesus and Paul are talking about judging those who are not citizens of God's kingdom (which includes Sam Harris, Richard Dawkins, and Christopher Hitchens). If we're supposed to correct or help any people out of their sinful ways, it's our fellow believers. And even then, we need to guard against falling into the same temptations (Galatians 6:1).

Lots of people who judge others and their behavior end up falling into the same sin they are protesting. Whenever you hear about the moral failure of well-known religious leaders or political figures, don't be surprised. But neither should you gloat. Don't get all self-righteous. Don't be driven by your pride. Pray for them and their families. And remember who you are. As the Scriptures say, "Though the LORD is great, he cares for the humble, but he keeps his distance from the proud" (Psalm 138:6).

Remember Whose We Are
Those of us who call ourselves Christians also need to remember

that we belong to God. With this in mind, our relationship to our culture—including the political process—should be as foreign citizens, or "resident aliens." In this way we are like Abraham, who was called by God to leave his home and go to another country that God would give him as his inheritance. "He went without knowing where he was going. And even when he reached the land God had promised him, he lived there by faith—for he was like a foreigner, living in tents" (Hebrews 11:8-9).

This doesn't mean that we can't be productive and influential in the culture—we've seen Jesus' reference to salt and light—but we have to always remember that our true citizenship is in heaven (Philippians 3:20). Gregory Boyd writes about this:

> Whatever opinions we have about how to solve society's problems, we are to remember always that we cannot serve two masters (Luke 16:13). Our allegiance, therefore, can never be to any version of the kingdom-of-the-world, however much better we may think it is than other versions of the king-of-the-world. Our allegiance is to our heavenly Father, whose country we belong to and into whose family we've been adopted.[2]

From time to time our heavenly Father may call us to do something in the culture, something that usually becomes clear after God has put us in a position of influence. Here are three examples from the Old Testament that illustrate this.

Daniel was an exile from Jerusalem living in Babylon in the sixth century BC. Because God's favor was on him, and because God had a purpose for his life, Daniel and his three friends—Shadrach, Meshach, and Abednego—were elevated to prominent positions in the kingdom. And God's idea was not for them to overthrow the government. God used these brave and dedicated men to witness to the culture that they served the one true God. But they had to undergo some serious testing. Daniel was dropped into a den of lions, and his three friends were thrown into a fiery furnace for refusing to worship the Babylonian gods rather than the one true God. God not only preserved them but also set the stage for the eventual return of the Jewish exiles back to Jerusalem.

Esther was the Queen of Persia in the fifth century BC with access to the seat of power. She was a Jew, which meant her husband didn't share her belief. In fact, he ordered an edict that anyone who didn't worship him would be put to death. The Jews living in this foreign culture couldn't worship him, so they were in danger of being annihilated. In this dramatic story, God clearly put Esther in a position to help her people. Knowing this, Esther's cousin, Mordecai, told her, "Who knows if perhaps you were made queen for just such a time as this?" (Esther 4:14).

Nehemiah also lived as an exile in Persia in the fifth century BC. Like Esther, he held an important position in the Persian Empire. Because of his excellent work and unblemished integrity, Nehemiah gained the king's favor, so much so that the king allowed Nehemiah to return with his people to Jerusalem. Even more, the king financed the expedition and granted him safe passage throughout the journey.

> "Who knows if perhaps you were made queen for just such a time as this?" (Esther 4:14).

These three people were examples of citizens of heaven living in foreign lands whom God used "for just such a time as this." Notice that none of them condemned the culture. None of them sat in judgment against the culture. None of them used their relationship with God as an excuse to take over the culture. They simply displayed the principle so beautifully stated by the apostle Peter, who also lived in a hostile culture: "Respect everyone, and love your Christian brothers and sisters. Fear God, and respect the king" (1 Peter 2:17).

At the same time, neither did any of these God-fearing people bow to the pressures of the culture. They weren't absorbed by the culture and didn't let the culture press them into its mold. They knew their true citizenship was in heaven, and their true King was God. And they obeyed and followed him even when their own lives were at stake.

How different could our witness be before a country whose inhabitants sometimes look at us with disdain? How much more of an influence could we have if we stopped trying to gain power but instead made loving and serving God and others our primary concern?

I'm Fine with God...

but I Can't Stand Christians Who Think Science Is the Enemy

In 1997 Bruce and I wrote the first in a series of Christianity 101 books that communicate Bible basics in a way that's clear and casual. The book, entitled *Knowing God 101*, addresses a number of issues about God that are important for any person seeking to know God: His personality, His written Word, His three-in-one nature, creation, the nature of humankind, sin, Jesus, salvation, the Holy Spirit, and the future.

Before long, we received an e-mail from a guy who was using the book in a men's small group Bible study. We were thrilled, of course, to learn that somebody actually thought enough of our book to include it in a study. But when our new best friend told us how God was using it, we were stunned. Evidently one of the participants in the study was not a Christian. The only reason he was involved was that he liked hanging out with the other men in the group. Each week the men brought their Bibles and used our book as a jumping off point to read different verses and talk about them. Not this guy. He didn't bring a Bible. In fact, he hadn't even opened a Bible in years. That is, until the group got to chapter 5 in *Knowing God 101*.

Chapter 5 is called "Creation: A Likely Story." Here's where we talk about God as Creator, explaining how a person's worldview is connected to whether he believes God brought the universe into existence.

We give a brief overview of the creation story in Genesis 1–2 and conclude by giving our view that the most important part of creation is the *who*, as in who did it. Next comes the *how* of creation, as in how God did it. Finally there's the *when*, as in when it happened. The only nonnegotiable in this group of who, how, and when topics is the *who*. From our perspective, the *how* and the *when* are open to discussion. (You'd be surprised how many Christians disapprove of that view.)

We make two other statements in the book that also get the attention of some Christians, especially since they come from two confirmed theists like us: (1) God made the Big Bang happen, and (2) "science" is not a dirty word.

These statements also got the attention of the man who never opened his Bible. The Bible study leader told us that on the morning they were going to study chapter 5, he noticed something very unusual about this man: He brought a Bible. The leader was surprised and asked him about the sudden change. Here's what he said.

> I never told you guys why I haven't opened a Bible in years, and you never pressed me, which is partly why I keep coming. You have accepted me where I am. Well, I can tell you now that the reason I never opened the Bible was that I couldn't get past Genesis. I couldn't accept the fact that God created the earth in six literal days and that He did it 6000 years ago. With everything science has learned about the universe, the way I figured it, if the Bible got it wrong in Genesis, how in the world could I trust the rest of it?
>
> But this past week I read chapter 5 in this book, and for the first time I saw that there are other options for creation. If I can read Genesis without having to believe things I think contradict science, then I think I'll give the rest of the Bible a try.

A Stumbling Block

I don't know what happened to the man in the Bible study. I'm comfortable leaving that to God. But I did learn an important lesson about stumbling blocks. We all know what a stumbling block is in the natural world: a physical obstacle in our path that trips us up and deters us from our destination. Stumbling blocks obstruct our spiritual journey as well. These conceptual obstacles trip us up and deter us from our destination of getting to know God better and better. The apostle Paul advised the Christians in the Roman church "to live in such a way that you will not cause another believer to stumble and fall" (Romans 14:13).

> With everything science has learned about the universe, the way I figured it, if the Bible got it wrong in Genesis, how in the world could I trust the rest of it?
>
> AN HONEST SKEPTIC

A spiritual stumbling block can take the form of behavior—good or bad—that throws someone else off. Paul talked about behaviors that are harmless for one person but can be a stumbling block for someone else. (An example of this is drinking a glass of wine in the presence of a recovering alcoholic.) A spiritual stumbling block can also be an idea or a belief—even one that seems benign—that confuses people and throws them off the path that leads to knowing God. In the case of the man in the Bible study, the major stumbling block in his spiritual journey was the idea that God created the earth 6000 years ago in six literal days.

From a spiritual perspective, this idea is pretty benign. It certainly isn't a core issue in salvation. But somehow this man had come to the conclusion that he had to believe the "facts" of a young earth and literal six-day creation in order to buy into the rest of the Bible, which means he probably thought he had to believe them in order to become a Christian.

Do you see what I mean by "stumbling block"? I still shudder to think about it. This man was faced with the terrible dilemma of choosing between an interpretation of Scripture he thought was absolutely false and a scientific position he believed to be absolutely true—with his eternal soul hanging in the balance. That's unconscionable. Yet stumbling blocks like this and the dilemmas they create are all around us, and well-intentioned Christians put them there.

I am well aware that some stumbling blocks exist because God has put them there. For example, the cross of Christ is a stumbling block to some people (1 Corinthians 1:23 NIV). That's not our problem. But when we are the ones who throw obstacles into the paths of fellow believers—or worse, searching skeptics like the man in the Bible study—then it is our problem, and we have to fix it.

In a way, this entire book is all about spiritual stumbling blocks. Most of them are ideas that Christians have made nonnegotiable even though they are far from the core of biblical essentials. The purpose of this chapter is to deal with one particular stumbling block that is keeping people from knowing God. This isn't just about the days of creation or the age of the earth, although it includes those topics. It's a bigger issue in the whole "science and religion" conversation, and it comes out of a strong position that some Christians take. I can't stand it. Here it is.

I Can't Stand Christians Who Think Science Is the Enemy

This is a complicated issue, perhaps more complicated than any of the other items in this book. As I write this, I'm surrounded by stacks of books containing more information on science and religion (or more correctly, science and faith) than I could ever synthesize and compress into a single book, let alone a single chapter. So instead of trying to do the impossible, I want to simply communicate to you in a way that is clear and casual why some Christians have made an enemy out of science and scientists. And I'll try to explain what God thinks about science and faith, focusing in particular on the way both of these disciplines approach the issue of origins (how the universe got here).

I happen to think that science and faith are not enemies, but we have made them that way. By "we" I mean Christians. Maybe not the majority of Christians, but Christians nonetheless. I am well aware that some very vocal non-Christians are equally guilty of setting science and faith in opposition. But as I did in the last chapter, I want to take responsibility on behalf of my fellow believers for starting the current fight. So I'm not going to spend any time answering the assertions of those who are opposed to faith. Instead, I'll focus on those who are opposed to science.

A Brief History of Faith and Science

The belief that God created the earth in six literal days—and that God did his creating thousands of years ago rather than billions—didn't gain real traction among Christians until the late nineteenth century. Many centuries before that, Bible scholars such as Justin Martyr (AD 100–160), Irenaeus (130–200), and Origen (185–254) believed that each day of creation was 1000 years or longer. St. Augustine (354–430), who viewed the Genesis account of creation as spiritual rather than literal, believed the days of creation as described in Genesis 1 were undetermined periods of time.

Throughout the first millennium AD, science and faith had little in common. But Thomas Aquinas changed all that. In the thirteenth century, he published *Summa Theologica,* which started a new conversation about science (represented by reason) and religion (represented by faith). Arguing that all truth is one, he saw these two systems of thought as complementary rather than contradictory. Aquinas also developed the classic arguments for God: the cosmological argument, the argument from design, the ontological argument (that all people have a God idea), and the moral argument.

After Aquinas and throughout the Renaissance, scientific knowledge advanced by leaps and bounds, and some of it challenged certain assumptions long held by the church. In chapter 1, we mentioned Galileo, who taught (based on Copernicus) that the earth was not the center of the universe. Galileo was a Catholic and did not believe his ideas violated Scripture. The church saw it differently and forced Galileo to recant his position.

The net result of this and other alleged conflicts between science and the church was the misconception that science and faith were not compatible, resulting in a parting of the ways. When Darwin published *On the Origin of Species* in 1859, that division was set in stone. Even though Darwin did not set out to remove God as Creator, his followers saw his theory of natural selection and common descent as a way to do just that.

As for the Christians, some thought Darwin's theory of evolution made sense, and they tried to blend it with Scripture. Others rejected evolution completely and vilified Darwin, deepening the divide between science and faith.

The Rise of Scientific Creationism

The Christian reaction to evolution and Darwinism came to a point in the development of scientific creationism in the late nineteenth century. This new movement emerged not from the work of scientists or theologians but from the visions of Ellen G. White, founder of the Seventh-day Adventist Church. White taught three principles that remain the bedrock of belief for scientific creationists to this day:

- the creation days were 24 hours long,
- the great flood accounted for the geological changes that make the earth appear old, and
- the Bible is a sourcebook for science.

This view led to the modern scientific creationist position that allows only one possible interpretation of the biblical account of creation: the young-earth, literal six-day creation view. Even more, according to today's scientific creationists, any view of the creation account that interprets the days of Genesis as longer periods of time and says the universe began billions of years ago instead of thousands is siding with "atheistic evolutionism."

As for those who believe in any form of evolution—and this would include most scientists and theistic evolutionists—well, they are clearly the enemy, or at the very least, unbiblical. Here's an excerpt from "Wrong on Two Counts" by John Morris, president of the Institute for Creation Research, the leading proponent of scientific creationism. Dr. Morris begins with a reference to an encounter Jesus had with a group of people who opposed Him:

> "Jesus answered and said unto them, Ye do err, not knowing the scriptures, nor the power of God" (Matthew 22:29).
>
> When the Sadducees, who were the theological, philosophical, and scientific elite of the day, came to Jesus with a trick question in an attempt to discredit Him, He responded with the stinging rebuke in our text. While His response dealt specifically with the fact of resurrection and the nature of the after-life, His two-fold evaluation of self-reliant scholars still fits today, particularly in regard to evolutionary speculations.
>
> By the time Darwin had published his book, *Origin of Species,* attributing evolutionary progression to natural selection, he had probably become an atheist and so set about to ascribe creation to natural causes. He attributed to nature, abilities which clearly belong to God alone. He knew something of the Scriptures, but his memoirs show that he had little understanding of basic Biblical teaching. He felt that if there was a God, He had little power or had not been involved in the affairs of this earth. Most atheistic evolutionists today follow Darwin's intellectual footsteps.
>
> But what of Christian intellectuals, theistic evolutionists, progressive

creationists, or advocates of the framework hypothesis, who claim to know God but yet deny His awesome power in creation? They too reject the clear teaching of Scripture regarding creation, relegating God to the mundane task of overseeing the evolutionary process, reducing His power to something potentially accomplishable by man. Peter aptly describes this attitude when he calls it willful ignorance (2 Peter 3:5).

It has been suggested by some that all human error can be traced to one or both of these categories: not knowing (and/or believing) the Scriptures and underestimating the power of God.[1]

Hugh Ross and the Opposition

Dr. Hugh Ross is an astrophysicist and the president of Reasons to Believe, a ministry that promotes a healthy dialogue between faith and science. Dr. Ross travels around the world, challenging university audiences, churches, and professional groups to consider the evidence for what they believe. He presents a persuasive case for Christianity without applying pressure.

I had an occasion to talk with Dr. Ross several years ago. I asked him where he got the strongest resistance for his views on God and creation, knowing that he does not embrace the views of scientific creationism. Dr. Ross said he receives very little push back from secular scientists. In fact, his fiercest opposition comes from scientific creationists who resent his views on the age of the earth.

The big problem with the approach taken by scientific creationists—or anyone who believes that one single interpretation of a nonessential part of Scripture is the only possible option—is that it leads to bad assumptions like these:

- Science is on a quest to disprove God and the Bible,

- scientists are for the most part opposed to God, and

- Christians who do not agree with the views of scientific creationism are opposed to Scripture.

Most people can easily see how unfounded and damaging these assumptions are. They aren't true (I'll tell you why a little later), and they destroy Christians' credibility in the scientific world. Even more, they severely hamper Christians' ability to participate in the faith-and-science conversation. Even though many Christians don't embrace scientific creationism, lots of people assume that all Christians do. We can protest that painting with such a broad brush is unfair, but we've brought it on ourselves. And it's time we make some serious corrections. In order to do that, let's find out what God thinks.

What Does God Think About All of This?

God is all about truth. Always has been, always will be. He is completely true in his character and always true to himself. As theologian Wayne Grudem states, God's truthfulness means that "all His knowledge and words are both true and the final statement of truth." This means that God is reliable and faithful in his words. Grudem continues:

> This realization should encourage us in the pursuit of knowledge in all areas of the natural and social sciences and the humanities. Whatever the area of our investigation, when we discover more truth about the nature of reality, we discover more of the truth that God already knows. In this sense we can affirm that "all truth is God's truth."[2]

The theologian (a person who studies God) and the scientist (a person who studies nature) have something in common: Both are seeking truth. And if truth is true regardless of where you find it, shouldn't the truth about God in nature (general revelation) and the truth about God in the Bible (special revelation) be in harmony? Of course they should.

The conflict arises when we draw absolute conclusions from insufficient evidence. This can occurs on both sides of the debate. A scientist might contend that *only* natural causes could account for the universe and everything in it. A Christian might assert that the Bible *must* be interpreted to say that God created the earth in six literal days just a few thousand years ago.

Clearly those two conclusions are in conflict with one another. But notice what is happening here. Not only are these two conclusions in direct conflict—one excludes God and the other includes him—but they aren't even in the same universe (pun intended). Here's why. The first conclusion isn't even dealing with the *when* issue because that isn't a debate among scientists. By contrast, the second conclusion is contingent on the *when* issue. In this view, saying God created the heavens and the earth isn't enough. It also stipulates when God created.

You can see the problem. Those who don't believe in supernatural causation are debating whether God even exists, whereas those who believe in a Creator God are arguing over the timing of creation. Talk about shifting the emphasis from what really matters to something so minor that we shouldn't even be debating it! Yet we are debating it, and by "we" I mean we Christians. We're the only ones arguing over when the universe began. As a result, we're not even in the real debate, the one that counts for eternity.

And here's the real tragedy for those Christians who are hung up on the *when* issue. They've set up a straw man that isn't even in the Bible. Worse, they are missing the opportunity to engage their faith with people who don't believe in God, some of whom are persuaded from scientific evidence that the universe had a beginning, which ultimately requires them to ask, who or what is responsible for the beginning?

> If truth is true regardless of where you find it, shouldn't the truth about God in nature and the truth about God in the Bible be in harmony? Of course they should.

What Does God Think About All of This?

So what does God think about all of this? To get to that, let's find out what the Bible has to say about the *who*, the *how*, and the *when* of creation, which includes the beginning of the universe and the days of creation.[3]

The Bible gives three creation accounts: Genesis 1, Genesis 2, and Psalm 104:

Genesis 1:1–2:3 provides the original account of the events of creation.

Genesis 2:4-25 recounts the creation from a different perspective.

Psalm 104 is a poetic version of the creation account told by King David.

Who

When you read these chapters carefully, you will notice that the greatest emphasis is on the *who* of creation. In Genesis 1:1–2:4, the name "God" and the pronoun "he" are used 36 times. In Genesis 2:4-25, the name "Lord God" and the pronoun "he" are used 15 times. In Psalm 104, David uses the names "God," "Lord," and "Spirit" 14 times, and the personal pronouns "you" and "your" are used 48 times. Clearly the who of creation is the most important issue.

Without a doubt, God—speaking through Moses in Genesis and David in the Psalms—wants us to know that he is responsible for the universe, our world, and our lives. We are to praise him above all. Notice that this doesn't tell us how God did his work of creation; it only tells us that he was the Creator.

> Let all that I am praise the Lord.
>
> O Lord my God, how great you are! You are robed with honor and majesty. You are dressed in a robe of light. You stretch out

the starry curtain of the heavens; you lay out the rafters of your home in the rain clouds. You make the clouds your chariot; you ride upon the wings of the wind. The winds are your messengers; flames of fire are your servants. You placed the world on its foundation so it would never be moved (Psalm 104:1-5).

> The Bible teaches us how to go to heaven,
> not how the heavens go.
>
> GALILEO

How

Next in importance is the *how* of creation. The Bible is not a science book, and God didn't inspire the human authors to write in scientific terms. But the Bible is trustworthy and accurate in the framework it sets for the natural world and how it began. The conflicts arise when we try to make the Bible say something it doesn't say. As for how God created the universe, the Bible gives us enough information to make just two definitive and nonnegotiable conclusions:

First, God created the universe by fiat—that is, by simply commanding it. Hebrews 11:3 begins by saying, "By faith we understand that the entire universe was formed at God's command."

Second, God created the universe out of nothing. There was no preexisting matter prior to God's act of creation. Only God could do this because only God is self-existent, which means he depends on nothing else for his existence. He is uncreated and has always existed. Hebrews 11:3 goes on to say, "What we now see did not come from anything that can be seen."

When

After the *who* and the *how*, the Bible talks about the *when*, but not in a way that makes it easy to determine. The first three words of the Bible, "In the beginning," aren't definite, but they are instructive. In Hebrew, the root word of "beginning" is "first," but the meaning isn't restricted to the "first moment." It's much more indefinite. Hebrew scholar John Sailhamer explains that the Hebrew word translated "beginning" refers to an indefinite period of time, so no one can say for certain when God created the world or how long he took to create it. "There is no textual reason why 'in the beginning' in Genesis 1:1 could not have lasted millions, or even billions, of years," he writes. "However, the word does not *require* vast time periods; it leaves the duration an open question."[4]

The same thing goes for the word "day" in Genesis 1–2. In fact, here the Hebrew is even less definite. It can indicate a 12-hour day, a 24-hour day, or a period of time not at all related to the sun. In one famous verse in the book of Psalms, Moses (the same guy who wrote Genesis) praised God with these words: "For you, a thousand years are as a passing day, as brief as a few night hours" (Psalm 90:4). And Peter gave this whole "day" issue his own spin: "But you must not forget this one thing, dear friends: A day is like a thousand years to the Lord, and a thousand years is like a day" (2 Peter 3:8).

The prophets were not hung up on when the heavens and the earth were created, and neither were the apostles. Why are we? We know the who (which is very specific), and we know the *how* (which is less specific), but we really don't know the *when*. God could have created the heavens and the earth in six days (hey, he could have done it in six seconds!), and he could have done it in six billion years. God isn't bound by time. The phrase "a thousand years is like a day" is metaphorical. Truth is, God is eternal and infinite. He is not bound by time. God lives in the eternal present.

> The prophets were not hung up on when the heavens and the earth were created, and neither were the apostles. Why are we?

Back to Basics

As Christians, let's stop arguing with each other over when the universe was created, or how long God took to create the earth. Let's set that aside and concentrate on the issues the world is really concerned about. And let's get back to essential truths about God that we can and must agree on if we are to call ourselves believers in the one true God. Here are five statements from Rock Harbor, a church in Southern California. I like these:

- God is a Trinity who exists and is the self-existent Creator of all.

- Jesus is fully God and fully human; He died for our sins, rose from the dead to give us new life, and will return again.

- Human beings are created in the image of God. We have each rebelled against God's kingdom and are in need of the salvation that he alone can provide.

- God's salvation comes to us through trusting the life, death, and resurrection of Jesus and is given to us by grace alone. Nothing we can do can earn God's favor.

- The Bible is inspired by God and is authoritative over everything on which it speaks.[5]

Gentle and Respectful

Just because we believe these essential truths doesn't mean we should unload our knowledge on the first seeker we find. Our goal should be to engage people with the truth, not to hammer them over the head with it. And in our engagement, we need to be gentle and respectful (1 Peter 3:15), not arrogant and demeaning.

While doing research for a book several years ago, Bruce and I interviewed Dr. George Smoot, an astrophysicist from the University of

California at Berkeley who led a team that designed and launched the Cosmic Background Explorer (COBE) satellite in order to measure the ripples in the cosmic background radiation. The purpose of the project was to look for evidence for a Big Bang creation event. Well, they found evidence for what had previously been a theory, causing Stephen Hawking to declare this as "the discovery of the century, if not all time." For the first time, science demonstrated that the universe had a beginning.

Rather than confronting Dr. Smoot with what we perceived to be the obvious—that a beginning implies a beginner, who just happens to be God, thank you very much—we simply asked this really smart and thoughtful man if this discovery had brought any meaning to his life. Here's what he said:

> I have had the time to reflect on what it means. The implications are big, but it's not clear what the impact will be. If your idea of God is that he is an entity in terms of a certain locality, well this is an awfully big universe, so if there's a God, then he has to be infinite and he has to be everywhere all the time. I look at it and I just marvel at two aspects.
>
> First, that the universe is understandable. You can test it and probe it. You can have a good understanding of what could have been very messy and difficult to understand. Second, how beautifully it all fits together. It's beautiful in an abstract sense rather than a personal sense.
>
> In other words, you don't get the idea that the universe is your mother. You get the idea that the universe is this wonderful state full of raw materials and activities and as a person, you're incidental. It's up to you to make your way in the universe, and to be amazed by it.[6]

Our interaction with Dr. Smoot is but one example of the ways any Christian can converse with someone who doesn't yet know God personally. Contrary to what you may have heard or read from those

Christians I can't stand, scientists are among the most eager to talk about the "meaning of life" implications of scientific discovery, as long as we remember two things.

First, science is on not on a quest to disprove God and the Bible, and scientists are not for the most part opposed to God. They are certainly not our enemies. Yes, some scientists and science writers have taken it upon themselves to remove God from the origins discussion, but most scientists don't feel the need to oppose God. Like George Smoot, they are truth seekers who are open to the implications proposed by their discoveries. What they don't like—indeed what nobody likes—are Christians who box themselves into a corner by defending to the death peripheral and unverifiable ideas about God and his world.

Second, Christians who do not agree with the views of scientific creationism are not opposed to Scripture. Rather, they are refraining from interpreting the Bible's description of creation in one specific way and squeezing scientific evidence into it. These open-minded Christians realize, as Don Stoner has said, that "both the Bible and the universe must be interpreted in a manner which does not contradict any of the actual facts contained in the combined whole."[7]

I am convinced that if we remember these things, God will use us to speak truth into the lives of people who need to (and long to) know him—whether the man in the Bible study or the astrophysicist from Berkeley.

I'm Fine with God...

but I Can't Stand Christians Who Are Convinced God Wants Them Rich

Christianity has always had its share of charlatans and hucksters. Why not? What other group is known for its characteristics of hope and faith and goodwill toward all humankind? People exuding these qualities make perfect "marks" for the con man. And so on late-night cable you can often see commercials (disguised as revival meetings) which elicit "love offerings" from the faithful and hopeful. For a donation of a mere $29 sent to Reverend Billy Bob's International Jubilant Ministries, each "ministry partner" will receive the Reverend's appreciation gift of a genuine splinter from the actual cross on which Jesus was crucified. This splinter comes complete with a Certificate of Authenticity signed by the apostle Paul and notarized by Moses.

Of course, a close examination of each splinter suggests that it once was a component piece of Ikea furniture before it was run through a wood chipper. And a quick glance into Reverend Billy Bob's warehouse reveals that he has stockpiled enough of these splinters to fill four railroad freight cars, indicating that the cross must have been slightly larger than the space shuttle. Though the splinter is a complete sham, a loophole protects Reverend Billy Bob from liability for consumer fraud: He can always counter that the recipient lacked sufficient faith to make it work as a source of blessing and enrichment.

> I can't stand those Christians, most of whom are standing behind a pulpit or a microphone, who promote a version of Christianity that is premised on the notion that God wants all of His followers to be financially rich.

And so it goes. Some sweet and innocent Christians are desperately waiting for God to change their circumstances. They are easy prey for entrepreneurial evildoers who seek to fleece God's flock with bogus devices guaranteed to produce a desired divine result. In their desperation, unsuspecting Christians are no match for the spiritual shysters who are anxious to collect millions of dollars of tithes and offerings in exchange for precious treasures like these:

- A tiny vial of healing vino from one of the urns that Jesus used when he turned water into wine.

- A swatch of fabric packaged as a Holy Spirit prayer cloth—actual pieces of the beach towel used by John the Baptist during his baptismal ministry on the shore of the Sea of Galilee.

- A Miracle Stone—one of the actual five pebbles used by the little shepherd boy David when he killed the giant, Goliath, with a slingshot. (Pick up your phone right now and have your credit card ready. This offer is limited to the first 100,000 callers.)

I don't have a gripe with the Christians who get taken in by all of this. When I see this kind of consumer fraud taking place, I have sympathy for the people whose plight is so tragic and overwhelming that they grasp for any shred of hope. I have a different feeling, however, toward the swindlers who take advantage of them. I concede that they probably won't get arrested for false advertising, so my prayer is that they get audited by the IRS, get convicted of tax evasion, and get sentenced to a prison where they'll meet a bunch of gang members, all of whom are enraged that the Miracle Stones they ordered didn't get them out of prison. Reverend Billy Bob could walk into the prison infirmary with 37 Miracle Stones shoved up his nostrils.

My sense of justice, like yours I'm sure, makes me outraged at the religious con men. But these are not the Christians that tick me off. No, I don't even consider these crooks to be Christians. Oh, sure, they call themselves ministers of the gospel, and they can wave a Bible and pound a pulpit like the legit clergy, but underneath that polyester suit with the purple satin pocket hankie, they know in their heart that they have no sincere spiritual commitment. In fact, they probably don't even believe God exists—otherwise they'd live in constant fear of being struck by a bolt of lightning for perpetrating fraud in his name. So this chapter is not about them. But it is about other people who probably consider themselves to be genuine Christians and who prey on the same kind of victims.

I can't stand those Christians, most of whom are standing behind a pulpit or a microphone, who promote a version of Christianity that is premised on the notion that God wants all of his followers to be financially rich. This theological doctrine just seems too easy, too convenient, and too enriching for the ministers who endorse it (not to mention too contrary to many biblical principles).

The Prosperity Gospel
Through most of the formative years of Christianity, wealth wasn't an issue. Granted, each congregation has a few people who seem to have a fatter bank account than the rest of the congregants. But for the most part, the financial status of Christians through the ages has been fairly representative of the economic level of the society around them. Throughout history, when most everybody was worried about survival and subsistence rather than wealth and excess, Christians were in the same plight. Eking out a living has been most everyone's primary concern throughout the history of the church. Like everyone else,

Christians were so busy scrambling to stay alive that they had no idle moments for daydreaming about a luxurious life. Only within the last few decades has excessive wealth become a realistic goal, or at least a conceivable fantasy, for lots of people.

Until about the middle of the last century, Christians were known for being hardworking. The Protestant work ethic was pervasive in our heritage. Idle hands were the devil's playthings. Yes, God was always present to help us in our time of need, but we operated under the basic premise that God helps those who help themselves (which is not a Bible verse, by the way). So we all worked hard. We expected the Lord's imminent return, but we also worked and saved as if it wouldn't happen within our lifetime.

In the mid to late 1970s, a new kind of Christian theology began gaining notoriety. Conveniently, television was becoming more prominent in the American culture and so the new theology was disseminated in large part by televangelists. Perhaps earlier attempts to establish this new theology by non-broadcast ministries had failed because they couldn't garner a critical mass in their constituency. But television broadcasts entered the living rooms of people who were susceptible to the lure of this new doctrine, and it found an eager and receptive audience.

> The new theology, now well-defined and clearly established in some circles of Christianity, can be boiled down in its simplest form to this foundational principle: God loves you, and He wants you to have lots of money.

This concept resonates with many people, and it naturally gained in popularity very quickly. For a while its momentum stalled a bit in the late 1980s when its greatest spokesmen were involved in sexual and financial scandals, but it has recovered nicely, and it now has all the credentials of a full-fledged religious movement.

The proponents of this false gospel often rally under the Word of Faith banner. Those who are more skeptical (or even critical) of the theology use a variety of taglines for it, such as "name it and claim it" or "the prosperity gospel."

Obviously, the prosperity gospel casts a light on God that makes Him look very appealing. Who could resist a God who wants to pour financial riches on you? You'd be a fool to pass up on such a deal. After all, the logic is simple. We're talking about the Almighty God of the universe, who says, "I own the cattle on a thousand hills" (Psalm 50:10). With all the assets of the world at his disposal, wouldn't he be likely to spread some of it around to his spiritual children? The leaders of the prosperity gospel certainly think so, and here is how one of them reportedly explained the attraction of her theology:

> Who would want to get in on something where you're miserable, poor, broke and ugly and you just have to muddle through until you get to heaven? I believe God wants to give us nice things.[1]

Obviously, this is a doctrine with much mass appeal potential. And mass appeal translates into an ever-growing fan base for the preachers of the prosperity gospel. This is now an outright movement that has a life of its own, operating almost independent from the rest of mainstream Christianity. According to a *Time* magazine poll, 17 percent of Christians surveyed said they considered themselves part of this movement, and 61 percent believed that God wants people to be prosperous.

The only thing surprising about these numbers is that they are so low when you consider that the promoters of the prosperity gospel have made statements like these to their eager followers: "Do you think God would have any trouble getting $1,000 extra to you somehow?"[2] "[God] will give you thousands, hundreds of thousands. He'll give millions and billions of dollars."[3]

But There's Always a Catch

Okay, it isn't quite as simple as "God Wants You to Be Rich." There is a condition precedent to God's financial blessings, according to the theology of the prosperity gospel. God is evidently offering a *quid pro quo* arrangement (Latin translation: "You scratch my back, and I'll scratch yours"). Bluntly stated, God wants to make you rich, but he wants you to get the ball rolling by giving money to him first.

This catch is not buried deep in the boilerplate of the prosperity gospel manifesto. It is not printed in a font so small that no one can read it without a microscope. People don't sign up first and then find out about it later. No sirree. This catch is prominently placed front and center. It is the foundational cornerstone for the prosperity gospel, and the movement's promoters are very open about it. In fact, they have done such a good job of disseminating this condition that it has become absorbed into the mind-set of many Christians, even those who aren't hard-core prosperity-gospel adherents, as evidenced by the finding of the *Time* poll that 31 percent of Christians surveyed agreed that if you give your money to God, God will bless you with more money. And why not, when the ministers of the prosperity gospel have laid it out this way: "When you give to God, you're simply loaning to the Lord and he gives it right on back."[4]

At first glance, you might think that the "give money to God first" catch would be a deterrent to some people. You might even wonder why the ministers of the prosperity gospel don't downplay this aspect of the program. If you are that naive, then I have a Miracle Stone I'd like to sell you. Yes, they might possibly attract more followers with an unconditional "God wants you to be rich" doctrine, but it appears to be in their own best interest to emphasize the "But you've got to give to God first" clause.

Maybe a little role-playing would be enlightening. Put yourself in the position of an elderly woman who is housebound due to her physical disabilities. Her meager disability and government subsistence payments are not quite adequate to cover the costs of her rent, utilities, food, and medical care. Her support group of friends and family is not able to help her with her monthly financial shortfall, so she is continually behind in her rent and juggling creditors and bill collectors. Without a job or a car, and with limited social contacts, her TV is about her only contact with the outside world. Because she is a Christian woman and constantly prays to God for relief from her circumstances, she watches television preachers whenever possible. Now, imagine her surprise when she watches a televangelist and for the first time discovers that the Bible actually declares that God promises to make her financially wealthy, and all she has to do in order to collect on God's promise is to give money to God. She is elated, not because she wants to be rich but because any extra income will give her the financial relief she so desperately needs.

If you were this woman, and you knew that you must make a financial gift to God in order to claim His promise of financial blessings, where would you send your money? To be official with God, it probably has to go to some recognized ministry (God might not count it if you gave money to a regular person who happens to be in need). But what ministry do you choose? Perhaps you choose the ministry you've been watching on TV—the one that told you about this "give to God, and He'll give more back to you" principle. After all, donating to this ministry is very convenient for you because the ministry has its mailing address on the screen, and a toll-free number is flashing if you wish to charge the donation to your credit card. And they even promise to send a thank-you gift if you send a donation. This is easier than giving money in the offering at the neighborhood church (where they haven't even mentioned the "give and then you get" promise of God, and where they aren't appreciative enough to send a thank-you gift). And so you skip refilling the prescription on your heart medication this month so you can send $50 to the attractive preacher on TV, and then you wait for God to fulfill His end of the bargain by sending big bucks to you.

Sad but True

This is not hypothetical role-playing. Sadly, it is a real-life drama that plays out whenever the prosperity gospel is broadcast, as evidenced by a feature story that appeared in the *Los Angeles Times* about a prominent prosperity-gospel television ministry. The exposé reported that lower-income, rural Americans in the South are among the network's most faithful supporters, with 70 percent of the contributions to the ministry's $170 million annual revenue made in amounts less than $50. One such supporter was interviewed—a middle-aged woman who lives alone and suffers from AIDS. She sends $70 a month to the ministry out of her $820 monthly disability check.[5]

I have no gripe against people who make donations to a charitable organization if they consider its work to be beneficial and especially if they themselves have benefited from the services of the charity. Without a doubt, many of the people who donate to the prosperity gospel ministries feel indebted (at least for revealing the "give to God and get back more" investment program). But I'm ticked off by the heavy-handed approach the leaders and spokespersons of these ministries use. They appear to be preying on the defenseless under the guise of praying for them. This statement is typical of what is repeated over and over by the hosts when soliciting donations: "If you have been healed or saved or blessed through [this ministry] and have not contributed… you are robbing God and will lose your reward in heaven." And if that veiled threat isn't sufficient to do the job, then it helps to heap some of the blame on Satan as one minister has been quoted as saying: "If the devil can keep all of us Christians poor, we won't have any disposable income to build Christian television stations."[6]

> They appear to be preying on the defenseless
> under the guise of praying for them.

Professor Arlene Sanchez Walsh, author of *Latino Pentecostal Identity,* has studied the effects of the prosperity gospel in the American Latino communities. Here is her assessment:

> The prosperity gospel offers a picture of an ideal life in the midst of neighborhoods wracked by poverty, gang violence, substandard education, and pervasive drug and alcohol abuse. Yet it rarely, if ever, changes the real-life picture in those neighborhoods.[7]

Purveyors of Plenty

If the analysis of Professor Walsh is correct and the prosperity gospel has no beneficial effect for society as a whole, then what good is it? Oh, wait! That's the wrong question. Instead, we should be asking, who is it good for? And the blatantly obvious answer to that more insightful question is this: The prosperity gospel appears to work best (and perhaps only) for the people who peddle it.

> I've got nothing against wealth. I'm all in favor of it. And I have no beef with people who have it, even lots of it. However, I am repulsed and angered by conspicuous consumption and excessive displays of wealth when it is acquired through the collection of donations from people who can't afford to make them. This is a shameful economic exploitation of the "have nots" by the "have lots."

The excessive wealth of the ministers of the prosperity gospel is legendary and well-documented. One newspaper reported the lifestyle of one televangelist of the prosperity gospel persuasion to include combined annual salaries for the husband-and-wife team of close to $1 million, use of the ministry's 19-passenger Turbojet aircraft, 30 ministry-owned homes, including two mansions at the beach and a mountain retreat.[8] This opulence is possible because the ministry is sitting on a nest egg of more than $250 million in cash and government bonds.

(Unfortunately, this bankroll doesn't deter the ministry from pleading for contributions from their cash-strapped constituency.)

Riches like these are more the norm than the exception. The big-time preachers of the prosperity gospel appear to suffer from the same malady: affluenza. Once infected with it, they can't be cured of it.

A Medical Anomaly?

Affluenza might short-circuit the synapses in the brain. Some evidence suggests that prosperity-gospel proponents lose brain function and begin to hallucinate that Jesus was equally materialistic. One preacher has gone on record as saying, "Jesus wore designer clothes. I mean, you didn't get the stuff he wore off the rack. No, this was custom stuff. It was the kind of garment that kings and rich merchants wore."[9] In light of this apparent gap in mental competency, ministry staffers may be busy looking for a photograph of Jesus in a three-piece suit to prove their pastor's assertion of Christ's fashion savvy.

The opulence of the prosperity gospel leadership is over the top, but they certainly don't seem to feel guilty about it. To the contrary, they contend that they are obligated to display such wealth. After all, no one would believe their message if they themselves didn't have the riches to prove the validity of what they are preaching. They must be the primary proof that the prosperity gospel works. How convenient.

Profess It and Then Possess It

Money is what gets most of the attention in prosperity gospel circles. As one leading proponent has written, "Many are ignorant of the fact that God has already made provision for his children to be wealthy here on earth. When I say wealthy, I mean very, very rich...It is not a sin to be wealthy."[10]

But the "you can have it all" euphoria extends beyond cold hard cash. The doctrine covers anything else that you might desire. It simply depends on what you want. Whatever it is, God will deliver it to you.

As I understand it, the default mode of blessing seems to be cash, but if you grease the chute properly, heaven will dump on you whatever you ask for. Here is how one minister has been quoted as explaining it: "If my heart really, honestly desires a nice Cadillac, would there be something terribly wrong with me saying, 'Lord, it is the desire of my heart to have a nice car and I'll use it for your glory'? I think I could do that and in time, as I walked in obedience with God, I believe I'd have it."[11]

But don't stop with a new car. If you declare what you want, speaking it out loud, your faith will be released by the words you speak, and you can receive exactly what you have been longing for: the healing of your physical ailments, the pregnancy that was previously inconceivable, the restoration of your disastrous marriage, and the cure for male pattern baldness. (I made that last one up.)

Forgive Me for Being Skeptical, But...

Maybe I'm cynical only because I'm a Christian who's not getting any of this "get rich quick" action. However, I prefer to think that I'm unconvinced because I have a brain and because I can't stand Christians who portray Christianity as a "show me the money" religion.

I just don't buy the whole prosperity gospel shtick, and here are the reasons for my skepticism. The theology of the prosperity gospel includes these problems:

- God becomes a means to an end. He is not the end in himself.

- Jesus didn't know how to work the system. If God wants everybody rich, wouldn't that include his only Son? Instead,

Jesus spent his entire life in relative poverty. Maybe that's the explanation—he was so poor that he had no money to give to God first. Or maybe the prosperity gospel hadn't been invented yet because there were no televangelists.

- Even if Jesus knew of the prosperity gospel but chose not to use it, his disciples could have used a few extra bucks. Why weren't they rich?

- Millions of Christians in the past centuries were deprived of this knowledge that God kept hidden for so long. (Maybe God needed the time to save up his money so he could have enough to fund the prosperity gospel in the twenty-first century.)

- Christians living now in Africa and China are predominately a poverty-stricken group. Why are they being left out of the loop on this? I can't stomach the notion that God's riches are available in special measure to American Christians as a reward because we've been so good.

- This is the only sermon that prosperity gospel preachers preach. They are always and only talking about "God wants to make you rich if you give to him first." You have to wonder if they preach this same sermon because this is the money-maker for them. Preaching John 3:16 would be nice, but it might not pay the bills.

- God is demeaned to the status of an ATM.

But above all else, the prosperity gospel is just too easy. Riches can become the reason for being a Christian. Even if you didn't sincerely believe in God, faking your faith would be economically advantageous.

> The prosperity gospel is Christianity's version
> of professional wrestling: You know it is fake,
> but it nonetheless has entertainment value.
> (I don't mean to offend professional wrestlers.)

What Does God Think About All of This?

Before I get to what God thinks, let me clarify (if you didn't get the drift already) that Christians of the traditional, mainstream camp are vehemently opposed to the theology of the prosperity gospel. They aren't jealous of the exponential growth of the movement; many mega-churches don't subscribe to the "you gotta give to get" approach. A pastor from one of the largest churches in America summed up the commonly held critique this way:

> This idea that God wants everybody to be wealthy? There is a word for that: *baloney*. It's creating a false idol. You don't measure your self-worth by your net worth. I can show you millions of faithful followers of Christ who live in poverty. Why isn't everyone in the church a millionaire?[12]

In every doctrinal issue that is hotly contested between opposing groups in Christianity—from whether women should cover their heads in church to the sequence of events for the end of the world—both sides can cite chapter and verse. We Christians seem particularly adept at taking verses out of context and interpreting them in a manner that suits our own persuasion.

The battle over God's endowment of riches on his followers isn't any different. The "preachers of plenty" do not enter the debate unarmed. They cite verses such as these:

- Deuteronomy 8:18—"Remember the LORD your God. He is the one who gives you power to be successful, in order to fulfill the covenant he confirmed to your ancestors."

- Ecclesiastes 5:19—"It is a good thing to receive wealth from God and the good health to enjoy it. To enjoy your work and accept your lot in life—that is indeed a gift from God."

- Malachi 3:8-10—"Should people cheat God? Yet you have cheated me! But you ask, 'What do you mean? When did we ever cheat you?' You have cheated me of the tithes and offerings due to me. You are under a curse, for your whole nation has been cheating me. Bring all the tithes into the storehouse so there will be enough food in my Temple. If you do...I will open the windows of heaven for you. I will pour out a blessing so great you won't have enough room to take it in! Try it! Put me to the test!"

- Luke 6:38—"Give, and you will receive. Your gift will return to you in full—pressed down, shaken together to make room for more, running over, and poured into your lap. The amount you give will determine the amount you get back."

- John 10:10—"The thief's purpose is to steal and kill and destroy. My purpose is to give them a rich and satisfying life."

The lawyer in me is anxious to argue why reliance on these verses by the prosperity gospel group results in contextual misapplication. However, this is not the place for it, and it would certainly be redundant in the ongoing debate. However, for purposes of this book, I believe it would be helpful to look at some overarching themes in Scripture and see God's character as it relates to this subject. Of course, I'll have to use individual verses to illustrate these themes, so I fully expect that I too will be criticized for the "pick and choose" scriptural defense. Nonetheless, I'll forge ahead, and I expect you'll be discerning enough to formulate your own opinion (which, of course, doesn't have to coincide with mine).

Divine Dependence

Our independent nature revels in the notion that we are self-made and self-sufficient. We feel important when we think we are in control and are masters of our own destiny.

> God is God, and we are not. He knows that, but we are quick to forget it.

God weaves constant reminders of his sovereignty throughout the Bible. Any inkling of self-importance or autonomy on our part is sheer pride. Rather than holding on to a false concept of our own importance, the Bible writers constantly underscored our utter dependence on God.

The more we acknowledge our divine dependence, the more we appreciate God's provision. We need to be continually reminded to keep this perspective because it goes against our nature. Our financial security is a personal and vital subject, but the Bible frequently reminds us to rely on God for our well-being rather than on our own ingenuity or the balance in our 401(k) account.

Here is how Jesus exhorted us to keep a divine perspective on our finances:

> Don't store up treasures here on earth, where moths eat them and rust destroys them, and where thieves break in and steal. Store your treasures in heaven, where moths and rust can never destroy, and thieves do not break in and steal. Wherever your treasure is, there the desires of your heart will also be (Matthew 6:19-21).

The apostle Paul gave a similar charge: "Don't worry about anything; instead, pray about everything. Tell God what you need, and thank him for all he has done" (Philippians 4:6). And in the very next verse, he explained the spiritual benefit that will be ours if we maintain an outlook of divine dependence: "Then you will experience God's peace, which exceeds anything we can understand. His peace will guard your hearts and minds as you live in Christ Jesus" (Philippians 4:7).

The tenets of the prosperity gospel certainly do not deny dependence on God; in fact, they affirm that God is the source of the stream of income. But God's role seems to be a mere technicality because the emphasis of the prosperity gospel is directed more at celebrating the receipt of the financial reward rather than worshipping the God who bestowed it. Furthermore, the promotion of the prosperity gospel seems rooted in achieving a high standard of financial freedom that is antithetical to any notion of dependence on anything other than one's own investment portfolio.

Sacred Simplicity

A similar but distinct theme runs through Scripture in tandem with the theme of divine dependence. In addition to wanting us to recognize him as our sovereign source for all that we have or need, God also wants us to disengage ourselves from the societal pressure to accumulate enough to become self-sufficient. God doesn't want us to be motivated by a quest to possess but rather invites us to live in the context of sacred simplicity.

> I tell you not to worry about everyday life—whether you have enough food and drink, or enough clothes to wear. Isn't life more than food, and your body more than clothing? Look at the birds. They don't plant or harvest or store food in barns, for your heavenly Father feeds them. And aren't you far more valuable to him than they are? Can all your worries add a single moment to your life?

> And why worry about your clothing? Look at the lilies of the field and how they grow. They don't work or make their clothing, yet Solomon in all his glory was not dressed as beautifully as they are. And if God cares so wonderfully for wildflowers that are here today and thrown into the fire tomorrow, he will certainly care for you. Why do you have so little faith?

> So don't worry about these things, saying, "What will we eat? What will we drink? What will we wear?" These things dominate the thoughts of unbelievers, but your heavenly Father already knows all your needs. Seek the Kingdom of God above all else, and live righteously, and he will give you everything you need (Matthew 6:25-33).

> God doesn't want us to be motivated by a
> quest to possess but rather invites us to live in
> the context of sacred simplicity.

The Bible reveals that God wants our thoughts and motivations to be focused on him and the love of others rather than ensnared in a financial success syndrome. We aren't called to consider money as irrelevant but rather to disengage from the temptation to make it a priority in our lives. Knowing that our default tendency is likely to be toward growing greed rather than sacred simplicity, the apostle Paul explains a pattern for us to follow:

> Not that I was ever in need, for I have learned how to be content with whatever I have. I know how to live on almost nothing or with everything. I have learned the secret of living in every situation, whether it is with a full stomach or empty, with plenty or little. For I can do everything through Christ, who gives me strength (Philippians 4:11-13).

Learning to live at the level of God's provision deflates the tires of the prosperity gospel tour bus.

Suffering and Sacrifice

The prosperity gospel renders any notion of suffering or sacrifice for God null and void. The theology of mainstream Christian thought puts God at the center, and we are called to do whatever is necessary for us to serve others in his name. In contrast, the prosperity gospel puts the individual at the center, and God is compelled to do whatever is necessary for him to provide the riches to us.

Sure, the prosperity gospel requires a little bit of sacrifice. You have to give to God first as a way of priming the pump of financial blessings.

But God seems to have a higher expectation of the sacrifice that is required to serve Him. Jesus Christ put it this way: "If any of you wants to be my follower, you must turn from your selfish ways, take up your cross daily, and follow me" (Luke 9:23).

You don't have to be an expert in ancient languages of Hebrew, Greek, and Aramaic to figure out that when Jesus used the combination of the word "daily" and the metaphor of "take up your cross," He was indicating that following God was not going to be a cakewalk. I see why ministers who promote the prosperity gospel don't use Luke 9:23 as their motto. Building a fan base by glossing over any effort and merely promising riches is much easier.

And perhaps even more specific to the prosperity-gospel debate is Jesus' statement that our riches might be the exact thing we must sacrifice for God. When a very wealthy man asked Jesus what was necessary to achieve eternal life, Jesus responded, "Sell all your possessions and give the money to the poor, and you will have treasure in heaven. Then come, follow me" (Matthew 19:21).

After hearing the answer, the Bible reports the man "went away very sad, for he had many possessions" (Matthew 19:22). Jesus didn't tell everybody that they had to donate all of their riches to the poor in order to follow him. He just said it to this particular wealthy man. Bible commentators suggest that God asks us to be willing to sacrifice all that we have for God. In the case of this rich man, Jesus knew that his wealth was his hang-up, so that is what Jesus focused on.

Here again we have a clear statement from God that won't be found in the promotional literature of the prosperity gospel.

When God Gives, He Wants You to Do the Same

The prosperity gospel has a cycle: You give first to God, and then God will give more back to you. It sounds great, but God apparently has a different cycle in mind: If God blesses you financially, he does it so you will be able to help others.

The prosperity gospel preachers wouldn't deny that you are entitled to use your God-given riches to help other people. But that suggestion doesn't have much appeal, so they emphasize how you can use the money for yourself. But God thinks that helping others should be the primary focus when he financially blesses someone. To help you recognize this nuance, notice the italicized words in the following verses:

> And God will generously provide all you need. Then you will always have everything you need and *plenty left over to share with others*. As the Scriptures say, "They *share freely and give generously to the poor. Their good deeds* will be remembered forever." For God is the one who provides seed for the farmer and then bread to eat. In the same way, he will provide and increase your resources and then produce *a great harvest of generosity* in you (2 Corinthians 9:8-10).

The prosperity gospel says, "God gives so you can get." But God's paradigm is this: "God gives so you can give to others." And that is why I can't stand Christians who are convinced God wants to make them rich. The conflict of interest in their theology has them thinking selfishly with their wallets and bank accounts instead of generously with their brains and hearts.

I'm Fine with God...

but I Can't Stand Christians Who Fixate on the End of the World

For all the controversy over how the world began, there seems to be just as much debate going on over how the world is going to end. But unlike the beginning of the world, which touches on the hard sciences, the end of the world belongs in the realm of mystery and conjecture.

That's not surprising. With origins, you're not dealing with eternal destiny or judgment or apocalyptic end-times scenarios. You're just trying to come to some reasonable conclusions about how the world and everything in it got here and what that all means. Whatever conclusions you come to, at least you're here. Not so with end-of-the-world stuff. When the discussion shifts to your future rather than your past, you automatically begin thinking about a time when you won't be here, and that can be a little unsettling.

Anyone who has even a cursory understanding of the Bible knows that the Scriptures—especially the book of Revelation—are full of references to a future time when the world is going to be a much different place than it is now. So technically, the world is not going to end, but it is going to be transformed into a radically different place, and God is going to be the one doing the transforming.

As I said, a lot of discussion is going on about what the future is going to look like, and as usual it's divided along the lines of belief or no belief in God.

A Future Without God

In general, those who leave God out of the equation believe that our world and the people in it are progressing to a better place, or at least they should be. God and the supernatural are not part of this view, so all that's left to work with is the material or natural world. Human beings are material, of course, so people will have to create this better world. That's why you see humanists leading the charge to clean up the environment. What good is the world if it melts away because of global warming?

Humanists also see hope for humankind in the way we all get along. Wars and violence are definitely a problem, but humanists like Sam Harris have found a way to explain this without blaming people. Unreasonable religion and fanatical belief are largely responsible for perpetuating and even encouraging violence and war. If we put an end to faith, we would eliminate the source of our problems.

But if you pull God out of the picture, you have a pretty big hole to fill. As Ronald Aronson writes in *The Nation*, "Living without God means turning toward something. To flourish we need coherent secular popular philosophies that effectively answer life's vital questions."[1]

A Future with God

On the other side of the discussion about future things are those who believe that God created the universe in a perfect state, but because of the human rebellion against God, things have become messed up. Consequently, life as we know it is in a constant state of degradation. Your desk, your body, the universe...everything naturally moves from order to disorder, and from more energy to less energy. Put more simply, everything that lives slowly dies. Therefore, the world is not getting better. It's getting worse, and it will continue to get worse.

Still, things are not as bad as they could be. Even though the world and its inhabitants are in a sinful state, God is in control. Under that control, the universe is orderly and operates according to physical laws. At the same time, the universe is an open system, which means that God can intervene and humans can interfere. We are capable of polluting our environment, which can affect our future. Such action is possible because the natural world is both orderly and open.

People with a reasonable view of God believe he is in the process of bringing history to a fitting conclusion, when he will make the world new and perfect once again. But the old one will have to pass away.

Even though I don't understand everything, I'm fine with how God is going to administrate his plan to initiate a new earth and a new heaven at some time in the future. I will give you my limited views on this subject in the second part of this chapter. In the meantime, I want to address my fellow believers and tell them why I can't stand Christians who fixate on the end of the world. Knowing that you can trust God for your future is important, but when you take your limited knowledge about how that future is going to unfold and turn it into some kind of weapon against those who don't believe in God, you do much more harm than good.

We have to realize that people tend to take all this business about the end of the world personally. More than any other topic of religion and faith, this one is a lot bigger than "I'm right and you're wrong." It's more like, "I'm going to heaven and you're going to hell." Even people who don't believe in hell don't like to be told they're going there. They take it very personally. That's why I am convinced we need to take a different approach when we talk about the future. But before I do that, I need to get a few things off my chest.

Puddy and Elaine

If you followed *Seinfeld*, you may remember an episode in which Elaine's boyfriend, David Puddy, gets religious and basically tells Elaine that if she doesn't stop pestering

him, she is going to hell. Elaine objects and berates
Puddy for his judgment on her. "What do you care—you
don't even believe in hell," Puddy tells her. In a statement that goes to the heart of our current discussion,
Elaine replies, "I don't believe in hell, but I don't want
you telling me I'm going there!"

I Can't Stand People who Obsess About the End of the World

For thousands of years some people have claimed to have an inside
track on how the world is going to end, because God has somehow
chosen them and given them exclusive information. The classic example
of this kind of special soothsayer is the weird-looking guy walking down
the street with a sandwich board that proclaims, "Repent! The end is
near!" I don't mind this guy. He's colorful. And besides, his message is
pretty much on target. It's the other extremists that get my attention, the
ones who get into all kinds of details and set specific dates for the end.
Here's a select "rogues gallery" of doomsayers throughout history who
were convinced they were hearing directly from God:

- In the third century AD, a Roman priest and theologian
  named Hippolytus calculated that creation had occurred
  5500 years before the birth of Christ. He predicted that the
  end of the world would take place in AD 500, or 6000
  years from the date of creation.

- In 950 a monk named Adso stirred up everyone when he
  speculated that the Antichrist would soon make an appearance. He didn't set a date for the end of the world, but his
  detailed description of the enemy of Christ set a remark-
  able precedent. Since that time, people in virtually every
  generation have looked for the appearance of the Antichrist
  (current contenders are president of Iran, Mahmoud Ahma-
  dinejad, and the king of New York, Donald Trump).

- On December 31, 999, thousands of people packed St. Peter's Basilica in Rome to witness the end of the world.

- When the Black Death killed a quarter of the people in Europe in 1347, many figured the end had come.

- Many soothsayers predicted that the world would end in 1666, which was the sum of 1000 plus 666, the number of the Antichrist.

- The Shakers, who came to America from England in 1774, believed that the end was at hand. The Shakers were antisex (no wonder they made such great furniture—all that creative energy had to go somewhere). They couldn't even marry, so if their ideas had prevailed, the human race would have ended. That was okay with the Shakers. The end of the world was at hand anyway, so the human race had no reason to procreate.

- The great American preacher Jonathan Edwards believed the Great Awakening was a sign of the coming millennium. Date setting is evidently not strictly the domain of kooks and frauds because this brilliant man actually predicted that the end of the world would occur in 1866.

- Hitler and Stalin were just two of a long list of twentieth-century villains who led many people to believe that the world was about to end. Also, the advent of the nuclear age in 1945 conjured up all sorts of apocalyptic images (not to mention hundreds of really bad science-fiction movies).

- Israel became a nation once again in 1948, prompting more than one prophecy watcher to predict that Jesus would return and the world would end within 40 years—or one generation—of 1948.

- In the 1970s, cult leader Jim Jones led hundreds of people from his California church, known as the People's Temple, to Guyana in South America. They established a settlement known as Jonestown to wait for the end of the world. In 1978 Jones ordered the members of his cult to commit suicide because "it was time." More than 900 people died.

- In 1988 (40 years after 1948) hundreds of thousands of people bought a booklet entitled *88 Reasons Why Jesus Will Return in 1988.* The book went out of print on January 1, 1989, and the author hasn't been seen or heard from since.

- And who can forget the millennium fever that swept the world in the year 2000. Those who predicted that the end of the world would occur at this time are too numerous to mention.

On a sandwich board in a city near you:
Repent! The end is near!

I Can't Stand Christians Who Claim to Understand the Bible's Cryptic References to the End of the World

In the fall of 1970, I was a freshman in college. That's also the year when Hal Lindsey's landmark book *The Late Great Planet Earth* first arrived in bookstores. I can clearly recall how that little paperback, which went on to become the bestselling book of the decade, changed my expectations about the future. Lindsey, a writer and Bible teacher, made a powerful case for believing that the end of the world was near and that Jesus was returning to earth at any time.

Prior to *The Late Great Planet Earth,* I hadn't thought much about the future. After reading the book, I thought about it a lot. Of course, being a college freshman, my thoughts weren't all that sophisticated. Rather than thinking about the implications of an imminent end-of-the-world scenario for the world at large, I thought only of myself. I wondered if the Lord would return before I had a chance to get married and...you know, enjoy the benefits therein. I wondered if the Lord would return before all kinds of bad stuff would happen in the world, such as nuclear war, the proliferation of Barry Manilow music, and the threat of even more Barry Manilow music.

Make no mistake about it. Like now, a lot of bad stuff and potentially bad stuff was happening in the world in the 1970s. See if this doesn't sound familiar:

- We were heavily involved in a war that didn't seem to have a purpose,

- violence was escalating between Jews and Palestinians,

- we experienced terrible natural disasters and feared more would come, and

- countries were threatening to use nuclear weapons.

With all this stuff in place, Hal Lindsey convinced me (and millions of others, evidently) that world conditions and events were lining up in perfect order and setting the stage for Jesus to return to earth. Lindsey's prophetic clock was set minutes before midnight, when the world as we knew it would end. Early in my freshman year, I remember attending a church service where Lindsey was the guest speaker. His message was so enthralling and seemed so accurate that on the drive back to my dorm, I actually wondered if I should finish a paper I was working on. After all, if the Lord was going to return as soon as Lindsey said he was, why would I waste time on something as mundane as writing a paper?

Well, as exciting as it all seemed at the time, and as certain as I was that Jesus was coming back that year, he didn't. For the record, I finished the paper, graduated, got married, and the world didn't end. Now, nearly four decades later, I'm still here. Even Barry Manilow is still around. Which brings me to my current point. The reason I can't stand people who claim to have the Bible's prophetic references figured out (including all the symbolism in Revelation) is that no one has gotten it right yet. And guess what—they never will because God hasn't given us enough information. Jesus said that nobody knows the day or the hour when these things will take place (except for God), so we need to take him at his word and stop misleading people with messages and timetables that serve no useful purpose except to sell a whole bunch of books.

Today the message being delivered by so-called Bible prophecy experts has shifted somewhat. One very popular pastor and TV evangelist says that the end-of-the-world events that will trigger the return of Jesus Christ to earth rest on the nation of Israel. He teaches that God will judge us according to the way we treat Jewish people. He even says that anti-Semites will go to hell.

I happen to believe that the spiritual nation of Israel has a major role in God's end-times plans. But I don't believe my salvation depends in any way on how I treat Jewish people. I believe my salvation depends on how I treat just one Jewish person, and that's Jesus Christ.

> The reason I can't stand people who claim to have the Bible's prophetic references figured out is that no one has gotten it right yet. And guess what—they never will because God hasn't given us enough information.

I Can't Stand Christians Who Ignore the Problems We Have Right Now

This falls under the category of "too heavenly minded to do any earthly good." Christians have always been accused of this, and in one sense we can't completely get away from it. As a Christian, I have a sort of dual citizenship. Yes, I am a citizen of this world, but because I have given my heart to Christ, I am also a citizen of his spiritual kingdom. I live in this world, but as one who follows Christ, I am not to adopt the world's ways.

I have a responsibility to align my priorities around God's spiritual principles, but I can't forget about my responsibilities to the world around me, and that includes a whole set of categories: properly managing the earth's resources, providing for my family and my fellow believers, and caring for those in need. I will be the first to admit that I could do a lot better in all three areas, but I am trying to be a good citizen of this world, as are many of the people who call themselves Christ followers.

But there are always exceptions to the rule, and they seem to get all the attention. And I'm not just referring to those groups of pious people who separate themselves from society in order to keep from being tainted by the world. Sometimes Christians can project attitudes of casual indifference or even hostility to the problems of this world because they are so focused on the Lord's return or because they don't want to be associated with the kinds of groups who are working to ease the world's ills.

Recently a group of 86 Evangelical leaders issued the Evangelical Climate Initiative. A statement in this document says, "Our commitment to Jesus Christ compels us to solve the global warming crisis." A number of prominent Christian leaders—including Rick Warren, pastor of Saddleback Church and the author of *The Purpose-Driven Life*—signed the document. In a move that could only be classified as Christians shooting their own, another group of prominent Evangelicals, including James Dobson and Charles Colson, issued a statement of their own that in effect criticized their fellow Evangelicals for adopting a position "on the issue of global climate change."

Without getting into the environmental debate, my point is that because of such disagreements among Christian leaders, secularists hold a strong perception that Christians could care less about the environment. That's absolutely not true, as evidenced by the Evangelical Climate Initiative. But some outspoken Christian leaders believe otherwise, and that just doesn't sit well with those whose citizenship is only in this world.

The perception that Christians don't care about the poor is an old criticism that quite frankly doesn't have a lot of merit. Critics like to point to the attitude that Christians have about this world not being our home (because we're just passing through). But they ignore the incredible work being done in third-world countries by faith-based organizations like World Vision and Compassion International or the amazing things being done in our own country by church denominations like the Southern Baptists. Beyond the good that faith-based organizations do, people of faith contribute more per capita to nonprofit ministries and relief agencies than any other group of people.

But those acts of generosity and mercy don't make headlines. The people who do attract attention (and then set the table for our critics to launch into a sarcastic tirade) are people like Clyde Lott, a revivalist preacher and cattle rancher from Mississippi. According to a report in the *Los Angeles Times,* Reverend Lott is trying to raise "a unique herd of red heifers to satisfy an obscure injunction in the Book of Numbers: the sacrifice of a blemish-free red heifer for purification rituals needed to pave the way for the messiah."[2] He hasn't yet succeeded, but his well-publicized actions feed the perception that some people get so fixated on the end times that they ignore the problems we have right now.

What Does God Think About All of This?

You don't have to do a whole lot of reading between the lines to discover what God thinks about the role of prophecy in our world. That's not to say that the prophecies themselves are clear or that God buried some clues in the pages of Scripture that tell us when and exactly how he is going to transform the world at the end of the age. But he has spoken quite clearly through his prophets, and that doesn't include the self-proclaimed prophets that run around today.

The modern-day wannabes don't even come close to the real deal. Put aside for a moment that many of them live lives of luxury and have their own television shows on cable. These false prophets fall flat on their collective faces in one very important category: accuracy. By definition, a true prophet of God can never be wrong because as a messenger of God, he must reflect God's character and perfection. In the Old Testament, if anyone claiming to be a prophet made a wrong prediction, even one, he was put to death (Deuteronomy 18:20-22). And you thought you had pressure at work!

A prophet's job was thankless and discouraging for one simple reason. Much of what the prophet did involved *forthtelling*. God called on him to protest current activities, such as idolatry, corruption, and injustice. The prophets actually spent very little time predicting future events *(foretelling)*. So you could say that the prophet's main job was to tell God's people what they were doing wrong. People today don't like to hear preachers nagging on them for their evil ways, and the citizens of Israel back in the days of the prophets were no different.

> A true prophet of God can never be wrong because as a messenger of God, he must reflect God's character and perfection.

A Message of Truth, Justice, and Love

As God's mouthpiece, a prophet spoke for God. So when you read the prophets, you can be confident that their message is God's message. Take the prophet Micah, who delivered a series of warnings to Israel from 742 to 687 BC. God used him to convince Hezekiah, the king of Judah, to turn back to God, as well as to announce the King of kings to the world (Micah 5:2,4-5). God also used Micah to deliver a message to the spiritual leaders, the ones who were "supposed to know right from wrong" (Micah 3:1). Instead, they were "the very ones who hate good and love evil" (3:2). God addressed them directly: "You false prophets are leading my people astray! You promise peace for those who give you food, but you declare war on anyone who refuses to feed you" (3:5).

Then God took them to task for their injustice: "Listen to me, you leaders of Israel! You hate justice and twist all that is right" (3:9).

Deception and injustice: two things God hates, especially when they are perpetrated by those who claim to follow him. He took his own people to task for their unfaithfulness in these areas, and you can be sure that he feels the same way today. The message may have been given at another time, but the principles contained in that message are timeless.

And here's something else you need to know about Micah and the other prophets. Even though Micah condemned the sins of the people, he never condemned the sinners. That's never the job of a person who claims to speak God's truth. Instead, we are to identify with all people, showing them concern and compassion. We may think we have all the reasons why people should turn to God, but unless we are willing to identify with people at the deepest level of their need, our words are empty and meaningless. The apostle Paul understood this when he wrote, "If I had the gift of prophecy, and if I understood all of God's secret plans and possessed all knowledge, and if I had such faith that I could move mountains, but didn't love others, I would be nothing (1 Corinthians 13:2).

How to Please God

Very often people accuse God of being a cosmic killjoy, full of fire and vengeance. It doesn't help that our current-day false prophets spend most of their time condemning sinners along with their sins. But that's not God's way. Yes, God wants us to obey him because he knows us better than anyone else and because he knows what's good for us. When we do what God wants us to do, we are living the kind of meaningful life he wants us to live. But God doesn't condemn sinners. He saves them (John 3:17).

So how do we please God? By avoiding those things that really bother him (like deception and injustice)? Well, that's a good place to start, but we also have to be proactive. We have to love God with all our souls, hearts, minds, and strength—in other words, with every part of our beings. When you love people, you want to do the things that please them. God is no different.

> When we do what God wants us to do, we are living the kind of meaningful life He wants us to live.

The people of Israel heard Micah's warnings, and they decided to change. They wanted to know how to please God and how to love him more. They asked the prophet, "What can we bring to the LORD... to pay for our sins?" (6:6-7). They wanted to know if God required more offerings, more gifts, and more sacrifices. But God didn't want their works and their sacrifices, and he doesn't want ours. Here's what God wants: "No, O people, the LORD has told you what is good, and this is what he requires of you: to do what is right, to love mercy, and to walk humbly with your God" (6:8).

Do What Is Right

Knowing what is right is easier than we think because God has built a sense of right and wrong into each of us (Romans 2:15). What's tough is doing what is right. Yet that's exactly what God expects us to do. If we do the right thing, God is pleased. If we know what we should do and we don't do it, God is not pleased (James 4:17).

Doing what is right doesn't stop with making right decisions about our own behavior. We also have to treat other people right. We must act justly in all situations.

Love Mercy

The definition of mercy is this: not giving someone what he or she deserves. That's what God does for us every single day of our lives. "Only the Lord's mercies...have kept us from complete destruction," wrote the prophet Jeremiah. "Great is his faithfulness; his loving-kindness begins afresh each day" (Lamentations 3:22-23 TLB). That's the attitude God wants us to have toward each other. When we feel like destroying someone with a biting comment or a hateful thought, God expects us to have mercy. When we feel morally superior to someone, God expects us to have mercy and think less highly of ourselves.

Walk Humbly with Your God

When you walk with someone you love, you don't walk ahead or behind; you walk side by side. That's what God wants for us. He wants us to walk with him in humility. Our natural inclination is to walk in pride, but that only separates us from God and others. When we walk humbly, we recognize that God is the source of our strength, our wisdom, and our very lives.

What Did Jesus Say?

Jesus made it very clear that no one except God the Father knows when the end of the world will come (Matthew 24:36). Because we don't know when the Lord is returning, we need to be ready all the time, for Jesus will return when least expected (Matthew 24:44). Obviously, setting dates is pointless, but what are we supposed to be doing in the meantime? Jesus said the most important thing we can be doing is loving God and our neighbor (Matthew 22:37-39). But how do we do this? And how do our actions affect our final standing before God?

Only one time did Jesus give any conditions or criteria for God's judgment. Take a look at what he said.

> But when the Son of Man comes in his glory, and all the angels with him, then he will sit upon his glorious throne. All the nations will be gathered in his presence, and he will separate the

people as a shepherd separates the sheep from the goats. He will place the sheep at his right hand and the goats on his left.

Then the King will say to those on his right, "Come, you who are blessed by my Father, inherit the Kingdom prepared for you from the creation of the world. For I was hungry, and you fed me. I was thirsty, and you gave me a drink. I was a stranger, and you invited me into your home. I was naked, and you gave me clothing. I was sick, and you cared for me. I was in prison, and you visited me."

Then these righteous ones will reply, "Lord, when did we ever see you hungry and feed you? Or thirsty and give you something to drink? Or a stranger and show you hospitality? Or naked and give you clothing? When did we ever see you sick or in prison, and visit you?"

And the King will say, "I tell you the truth, when you did it to one of the least of these my brothers and sisters, you were doing it to me!"

Then the King will turn to those on the left and say, "Away with you, you cursed ones, into the eternal fire prepared for the devil and his demons! For I was hungry, and you didn't feed me. I was thirsty, and you didn't give me a drink. I was a stranger, and you didn't invite me into your home. I was naked, and you didn't give me clothing. I was sick and in prison, and you didn't visit me."

Then they will reply, "Lord, when did we ever see you hungry or thirsty or a stranger or naked or sick or in prison, and not help you?"

And he will answer, "I tell you the truth, when you refused to help the least of these my brothers and sisters, you were refusing to help me."

And they will go away into eternal punishment, but the righteous will go into eternal life (Matthew 25:31-46).

How many of us have taken these words seriously? I have to admit that this is a relatively new concept for me. I knew this passage was in the Bible, but I didn't pay much attention to it. Only recently have I come to realize that when I help "the least of these," I am demonstrating my love for God and for my neighbor. I am still saved by faith alone in Christ alone, but the evidence of my faith is not in how well I know the Bible but in the way I treat those who are hungry, thirsty, naked, sick, and in prison.

Compared to the attention given to such end-times events as the tribulation and the millennium, this critical part of the final judgment is sadly overlooked. Maybe we need to take these words of Christ to heart because he's the one who's coming back. Come to think of it, there's no "maybe" about it. We definitely need to do what Jesus says, which means we need to spend less time fixating on the world to come and more time focusing on what Jesus wants us to do in the world right now.

I'm Fine with God...

but I Can't Stand Christians Who Make Lousy Movies

This chapter is mostly about Christian movies, but my concern extends to some of the Christians who are involved in related fields of entertainment and creative arts, including visual arts, television, and music. I'm talking about those who have one thing in common: They evidently consider mediocre talent and stunted creativity to be acceptable simply because it has a Christian label slapped on it.

Bathrobes Instead of Broadway

I'm not bothered by the local church Christmas pageant. Along with everyone else, I think those little four-year-old kids are adorable in their lamb costumes as they stand around the makeshift cardboard stable. And I certainly have no complaint with the three middle-school kids (two short guys and a tall girl) who are wearing fake beards in their portrayal of the three wise men. They don't look hokey because they're in a *kids'* production. It's cute when Wise Man #2 gets her beard pulled off because it catches on the latch of the fake treasure chest as she lays it in the straw between Mary and the manger. And it's even funnier when all of the little lambs start snickering.

I don't even mind (too much) when the adult choir presents its pageant of the crucifixion and resurrection story on Easter Sunday in period costumes and I can't help but notice that the Roman soldiers are carrying plastic shields and swords that are emblazoned with the *Pirates of the Caribbean* logo (because that was the only kind in stock at Toys R Us). I can laugh it off when the guy portraying Judas is wearing a Fossil wristwatch or the local townspeople of Jerusalem are wearing plaid bathrobes I recently saw on sale at Costco. I'm not even too bothered when the actor playing Pilate, who, in a valiant attempt to be pompous and dignified, is trying to speak with an accent. Apparently, he thinks Pilate is English, but his British pronunciation sounds like a blend of Cockney, Scottish, and Australian (with a hint of pirate).

Church drama is simply community theater with an offering instead of intermission. These programs are tributes to hardworking volunteer thespians and musicians. They are part of the fabric of America, and that is good.

But the efforts of so-called professional Christian production companies shouldn't be critiqued on the same scale and with the same graciousness we use to evaluate the Community Bible Church's annual Christmas production of *The Night Ebenezer Scrooge Met Jesus*. If a Christian production company is putting its art into the public marketplace, we should judge it by the same criteria we use to evaluate its secular competition.

> Christians need to stop expecting less than the best just because something carries a Christian label.

Divine or Demonic?

Christianity has a grand tradition in the dramatic arts. The Christian church played a big part in reviving music and the theatrical arts after the Dark Ages. Religious morality plays became common in medieval Europe as a means of teaching Christian values to the illiterate populous.

But from the time drama came out of the cathedral and ended up in

Hollywood, some Christians have had a difficult time with it. They like it only when it serves their own purposes and evangelistic agenda. They embrace motion pictures that portray the Christian message in a positive light (which happened more frequently in the golden age of Hollywood), such as these:

- *The Robe* (1953, four Academy Award nominations and the first movie filmed in CinemaScope), starring Richard Burton in the fictional story of a Roman senator whose life was changed when he came into contact with the robe that Christ wore when He was crucified.

- *The Ten Commandments* (1956, directed by Cecil B. De-Mille, winner of two Academy Awards, including best picture), starring Charlton Heston in the biblical story of Moses, an Egyptian prince-turned-deliverer of the Hebrew slaves.

- *Ben-Hur* (1959, winner of 11 Academy Awards, including best leading actor for Charlton Heston and best picture), dramatizing the fictional story of first-century revenge, redemption, life-changing encounters with Jesus Christ, and a blazing chariot race.

- *Chariots of Fire* (1981, winner of four Academy Awards, including best picture), based on the true story of the British Olympian Eric Liddel (the Flying Scotsman), who declined to run in a race in the 1924 Summer Olympics because his Christian convictions prevented him from competing on a Sunday.

- *The Passion of the Christ* (2004, directed by Mel Gibson; nominated for three Academy Awards), detailing the arrest, trial, and crucifixion of Christ, with a realistic portrayal of the brutality of these events.

The same Christians who praise Hollywood when it gives them a movie that they can use for their evangelistic purposes are quick to condemn Hollywood moviemakers who release a film that presents Jesus or Christianity from a perspective with which they disagree. Here are a few notable examples:

- *Jesus Christ Superstar* (1973, nominated for an Academy Award), a film version of the musical stage play that presents the last few weeks of Christ's life in an anachronistic manner.

- *The Last Temptation of Christ* (1988, an Academy Award nomination for Martin Scorsese as best director), presenting Christ's journey through life with human temptations, including a Satan-induced hallucination and dreams of a normal life that includes sex with Mary Magdalene.

- *The Da Vinci Code* (2006, directed by Ron Howard and starring Tom Hanks), depicting a professor who unearths a 2000-year-old conspiracy to cover up the marriage between Jesus and Mary Magdalene.

These Christians don't commend or denigrate a movie because of the film's craftsmanship, creativity, or production values. Instead, they give it a thumbs up or down based on whether the film's theme is for or against their theological agenda. To them, it's all about the message: If it agrees with their position, the film is praiseworthy. If it contradicts their position, then the film is demonic. Thus, artistic values are nearly irrelevant—which explains why these Christians have no qualms about making lousy movies that promote their doctrinal point of view.

Morality Moves from the Cathedral to the Cineplex

Perhaps the schlockmeisters of Christian flicks are indifferent to high production values because they are consciously or subconsciously jealous of Hollywood. After all, some of the people behind these substandard Christian films are the same ones who are involved in ministries that held prominent places in the culture several decades ago. Back then, their heavily promoted views on virtue and morality were in demand. But over the years, society has changed its appetite, and it now dines at a different table when consuming its mores. As these Christians see it, their ministries were serving a nutritious "meat and potatoes" fare of biblical morality, but now the culture is more interested in stuffing its gut with junk-food morals served at the snack bar of contemporary cinema.

This notion that Hollywood has stolen an audience that formerly belonged to Christians is not so far-fetched. Douglas Briggs, a former director of the Los Angeles Film Studies Center, has some very interesting opinions about the place and importance of movies in our culture.[1] According to Briggs, through the 1970s, the church played a central role in American culture. It was the place where people gathered and shared their beliefs and emotions with each other. It was a place that united individual families, communities, and the nation in shared views and values. But no longer. Briggs contends that in the last two decades, movies have usurped the role of the church. The cathedral of the present generation is the cineplex (those huge structures that contain 20 or more movie theaters within a complex and usually include restaurants and shops). The cineplex is where we gather and socialize. More significantly, our culture adopts the values it sees on the screen.

Society used to find its principles in the Bible, but now it looks to the entertainment industry for truth. Through films, television, cable, the Internet, magazines, and music, the entertainment industry provides the content that Americans absorb as their source of guidance. Some Christians are bitter about this reality, and they are carrying a grudge against Hollywood because of it.

Putting a Filth Filter on the Lens

Some Christians, with a disdain for all things Hollywood, assume a self-appointed role as societal cinematic censors. No one asked them to critique from this moral high ground, but nonetheless they choose to analyze, evaluate, and rate motion pictures. Taking a position of moral sanitizers, they scrutinize films by counting the cuss words, tallying the acts of violence, and tabulating the boob sightings.

This information may be helpful to parents of young children, but these groups take their mission to an extreme. Thus, a family-friendly film—not sanitized for your protection with a Christian label—was reported as "containing upper frontal nudity" for a scene that was nothing more than grade-school boys wrestling with their shirts off.

Unfortunately, Christian isolationists even base their movie recommendations on the perceived morality (or lack thereof) in the private lives of the actors of a film. For example, some Christians slammed the 2006 release *End of the Spear* for this reason even though it was considered a Christian film with box office potential. Look at this profile by the Internet Movie Database (IMDB.com):

> The true story of a group of Christian missionaries in Ecuador who set out to reach the Wadani tribe (a violent Ecuadorian tribe defined by revenge killing). When the 5 men from this group are speared to death by Mincayani and others in the tribe (who believe all foreigners are cannibals), the wives and children of those men move into the Wadani tribe to teach them about God. *End of the Spear* is an amazing story of Truth, Love, and Forgiveness.

This indie film had everything going for it to be recommended in Christian circles:

- A true-life story of martyred Christian missionaries.
- A well-made movie dealing with Christian themes of love and forgiveness.
- Winner of the grand prize for dramatic feature at the Heartland Film Festival (2005).
- Great acting. (Chase Ellison, who portrayed young Steve

Saint, son of the martyred missionary, received a Young Artists Award nomination for best performance in a supporting role by a young actor.)

- Christian individuals and companies were integrally involved in the production of the movie.

So what was the buzz in the Christian community surrounding this film immediately preceding its release? Critical acclaim with "must see" recommendations? Sadly, no. In the days before its release, some narrow-minded Christians were complaining that the actor chosen to portray dual lead roles had been terribly miscast. Were these Christians complaining that the actor lacked sufficient acting chops? Hardly; they acknowledged his talent. No, the criticism had nothing to do with his acting but everything to do with his homosexuality. On the very day of the movie's release, when Christians could have been flocking to the film with their family and friends (Christians or non) and later discussing the faith-centered themes of the movie, many of them were reading the following press release from the president of one of America's leading Christian denominations:

> The actor chosen to play both Nate and Steve Saint in the movie is Chad Allen, an actor well known to American television viewers for his roles in St. Elsewhere, Our House, and Dr. Quinn: Medicine Woman. But Chad Allen is also known for something else—his very public homosexual activism…
>
> Allen (whose real name is Chad Allen Lazzari) also speaks straightforwardly about his syncretistic faith, freely mixing elements of Christianity, Native American spirituality, Buddhism, etc…
>
> Mr. Allen…went so far as to suggest that his opportunity in this film represents a form of "bridge-building" between Christians and homosexuals…
>
> Chad Allen's activism is what many audience members will see, not Nate and Steve Saint.

Christians loved the film "Chariots of Fire," but the lead role of Eric Liddell was played by Ian Charleston, a gay man. Another great performance in that film was given by Sir John Gielgud, a homosexual man who was probably the greatest Shakespearean actor of the last century. Similarly, the role of Gandalf in the "Lord of the Rings" trilogy was played by Sir Ian McKellen, who has also been known as a homosexual activist. Yet, I was not aware of these identifications as I viewed these movies. Thus, the associations never crossed my mind.

Careful thinking is required here. We do not know what sexual sins or sins of other sorts may characterize so many of the actors, actresses, singers, music writers, authors, musicians, painters, sculptors, or directors we enjoy and appreciate. Christians are not called to conduct investigative hearings on such matters, and we begin with the assumption that all these, like ourselves, are sinners.

Furthermore, we are not required to enjoy or appreciate as artists only those who are Christians. Yet, we should learn to look for the connections between worldview and art that always underlie a work or performance.

So, what of the "End of the Spear"? Put bluntly, I believe that the makers of this movie made a very reckless decision in casting Chad Allen as Nate and Steve Saint...

In learning cultural discernment, Christians must learn to make decisions about a movie like the "End of the Spear." In this case, the problem was unnecessary. This controversy is over a member of the cast, not the foundational story or the larger shape of the project. It could—and should—have been so easily avoided.[2]

I can't help but shake my head at the irony. This spokesman states that he could enjoy *Chariots of Fire* because he didn't know the lead actor was a homosexual. So why does he issue a press release advertising the fact that Chad Allen is a homosexual, thereby making *End of the Spear* supposedly unwatchable to the multitude of Christians who might not have otherwise known this fact?

Not Sleazy but Very Cheesy

Some Christians are so afraid of Hollywood that they try to construct an alternate universe—just like Hollywood, but without the grit. Unfortunately, these Christians often have a sense of calling, but they don't have a knack for storytelling. If they are preoccupied with producing an antiseptic film, they risk producing one that lacks realism and truth. They have a legitimate spiritual commitment, but that may not translate into cinematic creativity. They may have Christian ideals but not dramatic vision.

When a theological agenda is the first and primary element in a film project, the script and cinematography are of only secondary importance. In other words, the film may make a clear statement, but it may be a failure as an artistic work. But many Christian loyalists will support even a bad film if it has been christened as Christian. The moviemakers can get away with it only because they are preaching to the choir (figuratively and literally). But if they want to get their message to anyone outside of their holy huddle, they should work on the script and cinematography first. If they don't do that well, non-Christians and discriminating Christians won't stay in their seats long enough to hear the message.

Stan Jantz and I spoke with Hollywood wunderkind Scott Derrickson about this issue. Scott was the writer and director of *The Exorcism of Emily Rose* (2005) and the writer of *Urban Legends: Final Cut* (2000), among other projects. You might be surprised that these films and others in the slasher genre were the work of a guy who studied at a Christian university before attending USC School of Cinematic Arts. Scott is a thoughtful Christian and an artistic filmmaker; he is not the kind that I have trouble with. We specifically asked Scott about how a Christian worldview can be brought into a film with the intent of affecting the culture. Here is how he answered our inquiry:

Anybody who approaches the creative process with that sort
of agenda is destined to thwart good creativity. You end up
writing propaganda and not something that is going to be
irresistible. Some of my favorite films are about honesty and
truthfulness, and you can't help but be absorbed in them and
find tremendous value. Christians have been guilty of not
doing that.[3]

Bottom line: Christian movies shouldn't be made—even though they are
Christian—if they have no more quality than the skits at summer church
camp.

Are You Really Inferior If You Just Think You Are?

I am fully confident that plenty of talent exists in the ranks of Christianity, but many of the most talented may want to keep their faith under
wraps. Who can blame them? Often the quality of the purely Christian
product falls woefully beneath the quality of what the rest of the world
has to offer. We Christians look at what the world produces, and we
are envious. We look at what we produce, and we are sometimes
embarrassed.

This is true even when the comparison is between movies with a
religious theme. *The DaVinci Code* stars two-time Oscar winner Tom
Hanks and is directed by two-time Oscar winner Ron Howard. Contrast *Left Behind,* starring Kirk Cameron (with production qualities so
bad, one of the coauthors of the bestselling Left Behind books sued to
halt production).[4]

And it doesn't help that the status of Christian actors pales when compared to those who have signed up under other religions. Scientology
has three-time Oscar nominee Tom Cruise and two-time Oscar nominee John Travolta. Buddhism has Golden Globe winner Richard Gere
(who manages to snag costars like Julia Roberts, Renée Zellweger,
Jennifer Lopez, and Catherine Zeta-Jones). Kabbalah has a celebrity
treasure trove with the likes of Madonna and Demi Moore. Judaism

could indefinitely provide guest stars to *Saturday Night Live*, with the likes of Ben Stiller, Billy Crystal, Sarah Michelle Gellar, Mel Brooks, Steven Spielberg, Matthew Broderick, Dustin Hoffman, and Barbra Streisand.

But Christianity...well, we've got Stephen Baldwin (who starred in *Bio-Dome* with Pauly Shore). And when Stephen discusses "a higher power," I sometimes wonder if he is talking about his older brother Alex.

What Does God Think About All of This?

Some of the radical Christians who are trying to promote their own films in an anti-Hollywood universe think they are making a difference, but they are only fooling themselves. They have an inflated opinion of their importance in the culture because they are too isolated to know what's really happening.

As we have seen in prior chapters, the approach of these Christians runs contrary to God's plan for Christians to be in the world and to be salt and light in it. I won't belabor the doctrinal theology behind this point. But you might be interested to know that a Christian cadre is making an impact in the film and entertainment industry. This is not an organized Christian militia; these believers have no shared agenda. Instead, they are simply individual Christians who are trying to make a difference on an individual basis by building relationships and producing excellent work that changes the industry insiders' perception of Christians.

Building Relationships

For successful screenwriter Michael Gonzales, it's all about relationships. Although he is well established in the industry, Michael knows a lot of people who aren't—the students in his classes at the USC School of Cinematic Arts and at the Cinema and Media Arts Department at Biola University. Michael recognizes a support network among Christians in Hollywood, but these artists do not shun work or relationship in the mainstream culture. Just the opposite. They are smack in the middle of it.

> It's easier to be a Christian in the industry now than ever, because the support systems are out there for actors, writers, directors, and technical people. If you're serious about being in the business as a Christian, you need to stay close to an accountability group of people who are doing what you're doing, and you'll survive. Little by little everybody moves up the ladder. I tell my film students that they are part of the cultural elite. The rest of the world looks to what they are going to produce. The opportunities are wide open to those who want to be directors and writers. There are positions available for those who are willing to work and build relationships. And it doesn't much matter that you went to the USC Film School. What people want to know is, "Are you real?" If you're real and there's integrity in your work, people will pay attention.[5]

Michael understands that some Christians have targeted Hollywood as a mission field, but he suggests a balance in the methodology between the work Christians produce and the relationships they establish: "The relationships come first, because if you write a script, you won't be able to put John 3:16 in there. It's just not going to happen. But you can make a difference in terms of how you conduct yourself."[6]

This is a refreshing approach for Christians, and it is catching on. (Imagine that.) It isn't pushy or threatening, and it doesn't jam Christianity down a person's throat. It is simply an authentic, genuine attitude toward faith that is reflected from a life well-lived. And the artist doesn't need to force a testimony or Bible verse into the artistic creation. Instead, he or she focuses on the excellence of the production. As a result, a dialogue about the quality of the work might stimulate a discussion of faith themes.

One of the leading proponents of this new style of evangelism is Makoto Fujimura, founder of the International Arts Movement, which seeks to unite artists who have a Christ-centered spiritual direction and encourage them to seek creative excellence. Makoto is world renowned for his abstract paintings using ancient Japanese techniques. Art critic Robert Kushner has called Fujimura's work "emotionally explosive." Makoto would say that his style of evangelism is as ancient as his painting style. He models an approach used by Nehemiah of the Old Testament, who was the cupbearer to King Artaxerxes. Nehemiah was able to win the confidence of the king because of his excellent service. Similarly, Makoto believes that he needs to create excellent work to impress the kings of his culture—the art patrons. Only after they have been impressed with his work will they be interested in the faith that informs his creativity.

> Unless I produce work worthy of my peers, I can't build relationships in the artistic community. Who you are in Christ and how you are valued by God is essential for understanding yourself. Out of that flows this point: your works express who you are. Then you must go into the community, and into the world. The relationships are all there. If art is communication, then it is a bridge to create relationships.[7]

Embracing the Industry

Christ's exhortation for Christians to be salt and light means that they must stop thinking and acting as if their faith (exercised in church) and their job (performed at the workplace) are disconnected. This is particularly true for Christians who have a passion for film production. They need an integrated view of life and should realize that they can be Christian in their occupation without making a Christian-labeled film. Rather than bringing quality films to the marketplace through an alternative studio system, they can work in the existing industry with excellence until they achieve a position of leadership, power, and influence. Some Christians are walking on this path, including Mark Zoradi (president of the Walt Disney Motion Pictures Group), Scott Derrickson (writer, director, and producer), Michael Warren (writer and producer of sitcoms, such as *Happy Days*, *Perfect Strangers*, and *Family Matters*),

Eric Close (actor on *Without a Trace*), and Patricia Heaton (movie producer and actor of *Everybody Loves Raymond* fame).

If all truth is God's truth and all artistic creativity comes from God (James 1:17), a Christian should not feel compelled to produce only work with a Christian label. God is just as pleased with—and society might be more receptive to—quality films that involve faith stories or that look at religious faith and values, such as *Chariots of Fire*, *End of the Spear*, *The Passion of the Christ*, and *Witness*. And spiritual themes can be found in films that do not center on a Christian protagonist yet that can deal honestly with issues that involve faith-connected issues (such as *Les Misérables'* perspective on forgiveness or *Bruce Almighty's* take on faith and free will).

The late Bob Briner was president of ProServ Television and an Emmy award-winning producer. As a Christian, he strongly advocated that the role for Christians was not to create an alternate entertainment universe. Instead, he suggested that they become "roaring lambs" in the culture by the excellence of their work. Stan and I had a chance to discuss these issues with Bob at dinner one night before his death. (Those last three words are probably superfluous.) He directed us to this passage in his book, *Roaring Lambs*:

> The number one way, then, for Christians to be the salt that Christ commands them to be is to teach His relevance, to demonstrate His relevance, to live His relevance in every area of life. We cannot accomplish this by talking only to ourselves, writing only for ourselves, associating only with ourselves and working only in the "safe" careers and professions. Being salt is not nearly so much about having more pastors and missionaries as it is about having many more committed Christian lay people thinking strategically about and acting on ways to build the kingdom in such areas as public policy, advertising, media, higher education, entertainment, the arts, and sports.[8]

Changing the Image

Do you wonder why the powers that be in Hollywood almost uniformly portray Christians in a negative way? Perhaps they only know Christians who behave in a negative way. Maybe they have no experience with thoughtful, articulate, and genuine members of the Christian faith who exhibit kindness instead of evoking disgust.

Believers who are upset that Hollywood does not portray Christians in a favorable manner should put down their placards, stop the protests, and call off the boycotts. It's time to try an approach that might please God rather than embarrass him. How about working in the film or television industry and giving the movers and shakers a completely different impression of what a Christian is?

This was exactly the point that film critic Michael Medved emphasized in a lecture at Hillsdale College:

> Why hasn't Hollywood gotten the message? The one thing this industry is supposed to be able to do is to read the bottom line. Why, then, do savvy producers continue to authorize scores of projects that portray religious leaders as crazed conspiratorial charlatans, when similar films have failed so conspicuously in the past? It is hard to escape the conclusion that there is a perverse sort of idealism at work here. For many of the most powerful people in the entertainment business, hostility to traditional religion goes so deep and burns so intensely that they insist on expressing that hostility even at the risk of commercial disaster. It's easy for most moviemakers to assume a patronizing attitude toward religiously committed people because they know so few of them personally. If most big-screen images of religious leaders tend to resemble [Jimmy] Swaggart or [Jim] Bakker, it's because evangelists on television are the only believers who are readily visible to the members of the film colony.[9]

From where I sit—on the couch side of the television and on the loge side of the silver screen—it's easy to distinguish between what's good and what stinks. When I see creative work at its worst, I'm quick to acknowledge that I can't do any better myself. But plenty of talented Christians can. And I am anxious to applaud them when they give it their best.

8

I'm Fine with God...

but I Can't Stand Christians Who Don't Know What They Believe

A lot of Christians think America is a Christian nation. Depending on how you measure that statement, it could be true or not. Let's look at a few possible options.

Some people say America is a Christian nation because the founding fathers were Christians.

If by "Christian" you mean a person who believes in a personal God who exists apart from his created world but is at the same time involved in it, then this would be a false statement. For the most part, the founding fathers were deists. They believed in God but did not believe he was involved in the world. God created the universe but then stepped back to let it run on its own. For example, Thomas Jefferson was not only a deist but also a naturalist. He once famously edited the New Testament, deleting all the supernatural events, including Jesus' miracles.

Some people say America is a Christian nation because our system of government is based on the Bible.

One of the foundational principles of America—that all men are created equal—is a biblical truth (see Genesis 1:27). But you would be hard-pressed to find any other direct biblical references in the founding documents. As deists, our founding fathers were very optimistic about human goodness and the potential to achieve greatness—even perfection. The truth is that the signers of the Declaration of Independence and the framers of the U.S. Constitution drew more from the ideas of the Enlightenment than from the Bible.

Finally, some people say America is a Christian nation because the majority of its citizens call themselves Christians.

Bingo! Here's one you can check off as true. Most surveys show that nearly 75 percent of Americans call themselves Christians. Roughly 50 percent of Americans consider themselves Protestant, and 25 percent identify themselves as Roman Catholic.

Okay, so by at least one measurement, America is a Christian nation. But somehow that statistic is a little unsettling, mainly because of the meaning of the word "Christian." Historically, the word has meant "little Christ" or "Christlike." In the early church, the followers of Christ were first called Christians in Antioch because they lived out the teachings of Christ. Claiming you're a Christian is one thing; showing it by the way you live is quite another. With that in mind, I think we would be stretched to believe that 75 percent of Americans—roughly 225 million people—are living out the teachings of Christ.

As we said in the introduction to this book, the word "Christian" has become so diluted—and to some, so offensive—that many people who have made a decision to follow Christ are choosing to call themselves "Christ followers," or even "Fully devoted followers of Christ." Presumably these are people who desire to be like Christ but are embarrassed by all the negative baggage that has come to be associated with the word "Christian." We can't know for sure how many Christians like this there are, but some polls have determined how many Evangelicals live in America. (Presumably Evangelicals are serious about their faith.) The number that pops up is something less than 10 percent of those who call themselves Christians.

What's an Evangelical?

Broadly defined, an Evangelical is someone who believes that...

- the Bible is the inspired and inerrant Word of God,
- the person and work of Christ is central to belief,
- lives need to be changed, and
- the message of Christ needs to be shared.

I'm in no position to determine whether Evangelicals are the real deal to the exclusion of everyone else. But from what I have observed over the years, I can safely say that many people who call themselves Christians—Evangelicals or not—often do things that are at odds with what they say they believe. Even more, their behavior is not consistent with the things Christ taught and the way he lived. To put it more bluntly, many Christians flat-out give Christ a bad name.

That's the topic of the final chapter in this book, so I'm not going to deal with it here. My purpose in this chapter is to talk about the Christians who, as far as the culture is concerned, fly under the radar. They aren't necessarily doing things that embarrass the name "Christian." They don't consider themselves morally superior. They don't hate Democrats. They aren't overly judgmental, don't get worked up when evolution is taught in the schools, and haven't bought into the prosperity gospel. Consequently, they aren't offending anyone outside the church.

On the other hand, these Christians aren't doing a whole lot to bring honor to the name of Christ. They aren't going out of their way to imitate Christ because for them, it's not about being Christlike. It's more about success than sacrifice. It's more about doing the right kind of things, not being the right kind of person. For many Christians today, it's more about knowing about God than knowing God. It's about knowing enough to get by but not enough to get better.

I think the reason so many people in America call themselves Christians is that lots of them have redefined what being a Christian means. More to the point, they have lowered the standard. Allow me to explain what I mean as I describe four different kinds of Christians I can't stand. And let me be the first to point out the obvious: Every Christian alive has at one time or another fallen into one or more of these categories. I know I have. So as I talk about these different kinds of Christians, I am talking to myself. I'm not proud of where I've been at one time or another in my faith journey, and I hope you aren't either.

Don't worry. This chapter isn't just about the negative. Help is coming. But before we can find a cure, we need to diagnose the disease.

> For many Christians today, it's more about knowing about God than knowing God. It's about knowing enough to get by but not enough to get better.

I Can't Stand Cultural Christians

Early in our marriage, my wife and I moved to Texas from our home state of California. If we had moved to North Korea, I don't think we could have picked a place that offered a bigger culture shock than the Lone Star State. Don't get me wrong. We loved the three years we spent in Texas. But it was a bit like living in a foreign country. Besides getting used to the Texas accents, sweet tea, rattlesnakes, and humidity, we were introduced for the first time to cultural Christians, or as they're known in Texas, Baptists.

The mid-sized town where we lived featured dozens of Baptist churches. We soon realized that having this many Baptist churches was necessary because nearly everyone in town was a Baptist. There were two reasons for this. One, being a member in good standing at a Baptist church was a requirement for being a good Texan and a good American (in that order). Two, being a Baptist was part of a good Texan's heritage. I don't know how many times we heard someone say, "My daddy was a Baptist, and my granddaddy was a Baptist, so I'm a Baptist." People weren't Baptists simply because they went forward on Sunday morning to join the church. They were Baptists because they were born that way.

My wife and I came to realize that being a good Baptist was also essential for having a successful career and social life. Church was where you met your friends, made business deals, and showed off your new clothes. In fact, next to belonging to a country club and joining Junior League, going to a Baptist church was the most important cultural thing a Texan in our town could do.

It's easy to make fun of Texas for having so many cultural Christians, but the truth of the matter is that cultural Christians live in every state and in every culture, and they all share something in common: They follow what Mike Erre calls "the suburban Jesus." This is a counterfeit Jesus who "would never be so offensive as to demand that we do what he says: he is more interested in the security, comfort, and prosperity of his followers. In short, much of the message of American Christianity presents Jesus as the purveyor of the American Dream."[1]

Well, that sure does sound like the cultural Christians in Texas—and California, and Washington, and Minnesota, and Florida, and Pennsylvania…you get the idea. It sounds like America, and I can't stand it, because I've been there, and nothing is more disgusting to God, as we'll soon find out. Meanwhile, I'd like to vent a little.

I Can't Stand Fundamentalist Christians

In the beginning, fundamentalism was a good thing. At least at the beginning of the twentieth century it was. That's when the word "fundamental," when applied to belief, meant "foundational" or "basic." It still means that in every other field except for religion, where the word has taken on all sorts of negative baggage. But that wasn't the case a hundred years ago. In fact, to help explain what fundamental Christian beliefs were all about, a four-volume set of books entitled *The Fundamentals* was published in 1910 and distributed to churches across the country. I have a one-volume collection of those smaller volumes, and I have to tell you, it's pretty cool. Written to combat "the inroads of liberalism into the Christian church," *The Fundamentals* defends the deity of Christ, the bodily resurrection of Christ, and many other foundational truths that liberal theologians had called into question.

What Were the Fundamentals?

Dan Kimball lists five fundamentals of the faith as they were stated by General Assembly of the Presbyterian Church in 1910, the same year *The Fundamentals* set of books was published:

1. The verbal inspiration (and inerrancy) of Scripture

2. The divinity of Jesus Christ

3. The virgin birth of Christ

4. Substitutionary atonement by Jesus

5. The bodily resurrection and future return of Christ[2]

Written by the top Evangelical theologians of the day, these "statements," as they were called, applied "biblical Christianity to the wider problems of life and culture by emphasizing the essentials and deemphasizing the nonessentials." Nothing wrong with that, even today, and I'll tell you why very soon.

But first I want to tell you what happened to the world "fundamental."

It got a bad reputation. Rather than using the fundamental truths of Scripture as a way to draw people to Christ, certain Christians of influence (mostly preachers) began using them as a way to measure and criticize those who didn't thoroughly believe them. And something else happened. The original intention was to keep the list of fundamentals short and sweet, but people began to add stuff to the list.

No longer was it enough to believe in the inspiration and inerrancy of Scripture. You had to also take every word of the Bible literally, even the symbolism found in Bible prophecy. No longer was it enough to believe that God created the heavens and the earth. You had to believe that he did it in six literal days about six thousand years ago. No longer was it enough to believe that Jesus is returning to earth a second time. You had to believe he is returning only after certain things have already happened, but before some other things occur.

In addition to requiring that people *believe* in a certain way, the fundamentalists demanded that good Christians also *behave* in certain ways: You couldn't drink, dance, smoke, gamble, see movies, watch television, or associate with Lutherans. Anyone who did those things was a "backslider" or a "carnal" Christian. (You may have noticed that having premarital sex is not in the list. That's because dancing was prohibited, and as every good fundamentalist knows, if you don't dance, you won't have sex.)

The classic image of a fundamentalist Bible-thumping preacher, pointing his bony finger at anyone who doesn't toe the spiritual line, has faded somewhat. But some Christians still think the only way to please God and get to heaven is to believe an extensive grid of doctrinal details and to behave according to a long list of spiritual do's and don'ts.

I Can't Stand Intellectual Christians

My father used to make fun of intellectuals. He defined an intellectual as "someone educated beyond their intelligence." As clever as that saying is, that's not what I mean by the term "intellectual Christian." What I mean is a Christian who knows about Christ intellectually but doesn't know him intimately, someone who knows about God but doesn't have a personal relationship with him.

The church is full of people like this. They learn about God the way they would learn about some other historical figure. They may even say they believe in him. But their head knowledge hasn't sunk into their heart, which means they haven't necessarily entered into a life-changing relationship with God. If you think I'm parsing words here, read what James has to say: "You say you have faith, for you believe that there is one God. Good for you! Even the demons believe this, and they tremble in terror" (James 2:19).

As Mike Erre points out, if mere belief in the existence of God is the standard, then the demons will be first in line at the pearly gates.

Certainly believing that God exists and believing the fundamentals about God is important (and I'm using "fundamentals" in a good way, as in "basic" or "foundational"). But if intellectual belief isn't joined by trust in God and the things God has said in his Word, then there is no true faith. It would be like going to an airport and telling someone, "I believe that airplanes can fly" but then refusing to actually board an airplane because you are afraid. You may say you believe in the airplane, but unless you confirm your belief by trusting in the mechanics of the airplane and the ability of the pilot to fly you safely to your destination, you only have head knowledge about airplanes.

Many Christians are like this. They believe God is real, but they are unwilling to entrust their lives to him.

I Can't Stand Illiterate Christians

I once knew a successful man who had an airplane with "John 3:16" painted on the side. He wanted everyone to know that he believed in God and his salvation plan. Evidently that graphic reference to the most famous verse in the Bible was pretty much the extent of his Bible knowledge (I'm exaggerating, but not by much). He told me that he had read the Bible in his younger years but not much since. "I learned all I needed to know, and since the Bible hasn't changed, it's not going to help me much to keep reading it." I guess he lived by the creed made popular by a gospel song in the 1960s: "God said it, I believe it, and that settles it for me."

Do you know any Christians like that? They're everywhere. They have entered into a relationship with God, yet they don't know much about him and really don't care to. Maybe when they first became a Christian they eagerly read the Bible and prayed a lot, but lately they've been busy, and they just haven't made their personal time with God a priority.

> The way I look at it, having a relationship with God is kind of like being married. Just because you tie the knot doesn't mean you stop learning about your spouse. Marriage is a lifelong process of getting to know the one you love better and better. So it is with God.

I will be the first to admit that making time for regular Bible study takes effort, and I haven't always been consistent. But over the years I've done my best—often asking God to help me—to learn more about him by reading the Bible and by reading books about God and the Bible. The way I look at it, having a relationship with God is kind of like being married. Just because you tie the knot doesn't mean you stop learning about your spouse. Marriage is a lifelong process of getting to know the one you love better and better. So it is with God. If we really love him, why would we not want to get to know him better and better? It's puzzling to me that some Christians "tie the knot" with God and then put him on a shelf to admire and call on when a crisis arises, when in fact they could be getting to know God intimately, discovering with great joy how wonderful, loving, caring, and majestic God really is.

As I said earlier, knowledge alone is not enough to have a personal relationship with God, but knowledge is essential. The primary way we gain knowledge about God is through the Bible. So if we don't know the Bible, we don't know God. The sad fact is that many Christians don't know the Bible very well. To put it bluntly, they are biblically illiterate. Maybe that's why a George Barna survey has shown that less than 10 percent of all Christians possess a "biblical worldview." What that means is that less than one in ten people who claim to be Christians rely on the Bible as a guide for their decision making or behavior. Instead, they rely on what Bruce has often referred to as "gastrointestinal theology." They depend on what they feel in their gut to be true rather than what the Bible says is true.

Survey Says

A group of incoming freshman at a prominent Christian college was asked a series of questions to test their biblical literacy. Here are some of the results:

- One-third could not put the following in order: Abraham, the Old Testament prophets, the death of Christ, and Pentecost.

- One-third could not identify Matthew as an apostle from a list of New Testament names.

- When asked to locate the biblical book supplying a given story, one-third could not find Paul's travels in Acts, half did not know that the Christmas story was in Matthew, half did not know that the Passover story was in Exodus.[3]

What Does God Think About All of This?

I think it's interesting that in all these issues we're talking about in this book, finding out what God thinks isn't all that difficult. We just have to ask him. We can do this a couple of ways. We can pray and ask God to tell us what he thinks. Hey, this isn't such a crazy idea. If you are a Christian, you have a relationship with God that is both spiritual and supernatural. That means you have the Spirit of God (that would be the Holy Spirit) living in you, giving you wisdom and understanding that go beyond "the kind of wisdom that belongs to this world" (1 Corinthians 2:6). Prayer is how you access this spiritual wisdom. That's why Paul wrote to the Christians living in Ephesus, "I pray for you constantly, asking God, the glorious Father of our Lord Jesus Christ, to give you spiritual wisdom and insight so that you might grow in your knowledge of God" (Ephesians 1:16-17).

The other way to find out what God is thinking is to "search the Scriptures." It's also a great way to find out what God wants us to do. As Paul wrote to his disciple, Timothy, "All Scripture is inspired by God and is useful to teach us what is true and to make us realize what is wrong in our lives. It corrects us when we are wrong and teaches us to do what is right" (2 Timothy 3:16).

With that in mind, let's get God's prescription for our problems. Let's find out what he wants us to do.

God Wants Us to Be Countercultural Christians

I grew up in a Christian subculture. My family owned a chain of Christian bookstores where Christians came to buy Christian products. My father also owned a Christian radio station, which played Christian music and aired Christian programming for the benefit of Christian listeners. My parents made sure I attended church from the time I was on the cradle roll (for the uninitiated, that's a list of babies in the church nursery). I went to a Christian college, and after I graduated, I worked in the family business. For the last ten years, I have been writing Christian books. I still attend church and even teach a Bible study for other Christians.

You may think I'm going to go on some kind of rant over my Christian subcultural experience, but I'm not. Far from resenting my life so far, I am extremely grateful for the family, the family business, the churches, and the writing that have been important parts of my life. I've been privileged. God has been extremely good to me, and I'm humbled to think of the way he has blessed me. I don't deserve my life.

However, I will tell you that recently God has been working on me, first to show me that I've been falling far short of what he wants for me and then to challenge me to get out of the Christian subculture from time to time and live in a way that runs counter to the culture around me. Throughout this chapter, I have been alluding to Mike Erre's powerful book *The Jesus of Suburbia* because God has been using it to work on me. Through Mike's book, God has showed me that by spending nearly all of my time in the Christian subculture, I am doing two things:

- I am separating myself from the world, something Jesus told His followers not to do (John 17:15). I may be really good at attracting other Christians to the things I am doing—selling Bibles, writing books, teaching classes at church—but I'm not very good at touching the larger culture around me, a culture that includes my neighbors and all the people I encounter on a daily basis.

- I am sometimes absorbed by the culture in the way I adopt its values. If I am simply living my life in a way that doesn't speak of my relationship with Jesus Christ, what good am I, spiritually speaking?

So what am I supposed to do? How should I relate to the culture? Mike encourages Christians to "form countercultural communities in the midst of despair and evil and to engage the culture around us."[4] For me, this doesn't mean that I stand in judgment of culture. Rather, I need to show the love and grace of Christ wherever I am. The best way I can do this is through conversation with people in the culture "out there"—at the bank, in the grocery store, at Barnes & Noble, in restaurants, at Kinkos, in cabs, at hotels, and anywhere else where I go about my daily life.

Here's how Paul put it: "Live wisely among those who are not believers, and make the most of every opportunity. Let your conversation be gracious and attractive so that you will have the right response for everyone" (Colossians 4:5-6).

I am being very transparent when I tell you that my conversation isn't always gracious and effective. In fact, it can be surprisingly critical and destructive. Hardly Christlike. The cure for me is not to start carrying a Bible around, showing people verses on the love of Christ. I need to be a living Bible to the people I meet, showing them the love of Christ through my words and deeds. I need to realize that I may be the only picture of Christ they may see on any given day. That's an amazing privilege, but it's also a huge responsibility.

When I criticize and find fault in those who are not believers, I am buying into the culture. When I communicate Christ's love and grace through my words and actions, I am living in a way that's countercultural. And I am living in a way that invites people to ask me about my faith.

Jesus was a countercultural revolutionary, not because he came to topple corrupt governments and condemn sinners but because he came to demonstrate the love of God in a most profound and personal way. That's what Jesus is asking me to do, and I'm pretty sure it's what he is asking you to do.

God Wants Us to Be Gracious Christians

Here's another word for the kind of fundamentalism I described earlier: "legalism." It's trying to win God's favor by doing certain things or believing a certain way and then expecting others to do the same thing. Legalism is never helpful in our relationship with God, not because good works or good behavior are wrong but because legalism replaces Christ. The gospel of Christ is the gospel of grace. We are unable to meet God's perfect standard ourselves (this is the standard required for salvation—see Romans 3:23), so we need Christ, who lived a perfect life on our behalf and then died in our place in order to absorb the penalty for falling short of God's standard. We did nothing to deserve it. It's by the grace of God, as Paul makes clear: "God saved you by his grace when you believed. And you can't take credit for this; it is a gift from God. Salvation is not a reward for the good things we have done, so none of us can boast about it" (Ephesians 2:8-9).

Because we have been saved by grace, we are the least qualified to hold people up to God's standard, or even more, to the standards we add to God's short list. Mike Erre explains it this way:

> Throughout the Scriptures, the people of God continually succumb to the temptation to draw the boundary lines of faith more narrowly than what God has commanded. God's boundaries are simply broader and wider and higher and deeper than ours, so he calls his followers to be marked by the center—their faith in Jesus Christ—rather than by their boundaries.[5]

Just as the writers of *The Fundamentals* did a hundred years ago, we need to emphasize the essentials and de-emphasize the nonessentials. We need to be gracious in the way we treat those who are showing an interest in Jesus.

> In essential things, unity;
> in nonessentials, liberty; in all things, charity.
>
> PHILIPP MELANCHTHON

Do you know why so many Christians seem unhappy? They're trying to gain God's favor by doing just the right things. This is what happened to the Christians in Galatia. Even though they had embraced the gospel of grace when Paul first brought them the good news about Christ, they had turned to a gospel of works. They were wrong, and they were also miserable. "Where is that joyful and grateful spirit you felt then?" Paul asked (Galatians 4:15).

Joy comes from a spiritual source; it's deep and abiding. It comes from within and is produced when we understand that God has been gracious to us and that he is the source of our peace and contentment, regardless of the circumstances. When legalism invades our lives, joy disappears. By contrast, when we live as gracious Christians, true joy is present and sticks with us no matter what happens.

God Wants Us to Be Transformed Christians

I mentioned earlier that faith is a combination of belief and trust. It's believing in God, believing that what God said in his Word is true, and entrusting yourself to him. When you exercise faith in this way, you become a Christian, not because of something you do but because of something God does in you.

"This means that anyone who belongs to Christ has become a new person. They are not the same any more, for the old life is gone. A new life has begun!" (2 Corinthians 5:17). Paul is describing a transformation from an old life characterized by sin to a new life characterized by grace, made possible by the person and work of Christ. That's what being saved means.

What a contrast from the way intellectual Christians view salvation. For them, it's a matter of agreeing to a set of beliefs about God. Mike Erre calls this having a relationship with information rather than with the resurrected Christ. God doesn't want us to simply agree to a set of ideas. He wants us to be transformed.

Actually, Christians experience two kinds of transformation. The first one—the one Paul describes in 2 Corinthians—is accomplished by God once and for all through Christ and the indwelling Holy Spirit. The other kind of transformation is ongoing, and it happens only as we operate in the power of the Holy Spirit. Indeed, we are commanded to undergo this transformation from people dominated by the culture to people dominated by the indwelling Spirit of God. Here's how Paul put it: "Don't copy the behavior and customs of this world, but let God transform you into a new person by changing the way you think. Then you will learn to know God's will for you, which is good and pleasing and perfect" (Romans 12:2).

According to Dallas Willard, this transformation occurs in the process of spiritual formation. Although this is something we can't do on our own power, we need to take responsibility for it. Willard says that spiritual formation is essentially the transformation of the self, and it works through transformation of thought, feelings, social relations, the body, and the soul. In other words, we are responsible to invite God to transform us in every dimension of our lives.

> Live your life the way Jesus would live your
> life if He had your life to live.
>
> DALLAS WILLARD

God Wants Us to Be Disciples of Jesus

A lot of Christians think discipleship is for super-spiritual Christians. After all, weren't the original 12 disciples an elite group who were devoted to serving Jesus full-time while the rest were just known as his followers? It's true that Jesus called 12 men to be his closest followers, but by no means was this an exclusive club. In truth, God wants every one of his spiritual children to be a disciple of his Son, Jesus. A disciple is simply a learner or student. So a disciple of Jesus is someone who learns from him.

I said earlier that there are a lot of biblically illiterate Christians out there, and that's very distressing. The Bible is God's personal message to us. It contains his plan to bring us back to a right relationship with him through Christ, who is the visible image of the invisible God

(Colossians 1:15). Why would we not want to learn about God's plan and God's Son from this guidebook for life called the Bible?

You would never think of making a trip to Europe without reading a guidebook. A star football player would never consider playing the game without studying the playbook. An honor student would never prepare for an important test without poring over the textbook. So what makes us Christians, who have a personal relationship with the Creator of the universe, even think about going through life without reading and studying the Bible?

"The longer you look at Jesus," said N.T. Wright, "the more you will want to serve him in this world." In fact, Jesus doesn't leave you an option. Like he did to those 12 ordinary men in first-century Palestine, he is calling you now—regardless of who you are or where you live—to follow him into a life of discipleship. Of course, how you respond to that call is up to you, but I can't possibly imagine anything more important for you to do.

I'm Fine with God...

but I Can't Stand Christians Who Think They Have a Monopoly on Truth

When I was a kid there were only two religions: Protestantism and Catholicism. At least that was the world from my perspective. I grew up in central California, which felt more like Kansas than the middle of California. Surrounded by farmland and filled with churches, my hometown was like a scene from *Happy Days*.

All of my friends were either Protestants or Catholics. That doesn't mean they all went to church on a regular basis, but they believed in God and knew the names of the big churches in town. Because my family owned the biggest Christian bookstore in the area, I probably had a greater familiarity with—if not an understanding of—the various churches. I knew that being a Protestant meant that you were a Baptist, a Presbyterian, a Methodist, a Nazarene, a Pentecostal, or a member of one of the other denominations that were around then.

My dad used to regularly send out catalogs and flyers to the churches within a hundred miles of our store, and on Saturdays he recruited me to operate an "Addressograph" machine that stamped addresses on the mailers. It was a boring job, so I passed the time by trying to memorize the church names. To this day I could probably make a comprehensive list of most of those churches: Memorial Baptist, St. Luke's Methodist, First Presbyterian (not to be confused with Calvary

Presbyterian), First Baptist, St. Mark's Episcopalian, First Church of the Nazarene, the People's Church, and so on.

We didn't send mailers to Catholic churches, and I don't think we had many Catholic customers because the Catholics had their own bookstore. The owner of that store and my dad got along just fine, mainly because they weren't competitors. Still, the one time I remember going into the Catholic store, I felt like I was in another country. I couldn't relate to all the statuary and the rosaries and seeing Christ on a cross. Besides that experience, my knowledge of Catholic doctrine and practice was limited to this: Catholics didn't eat meat on Fridays. The only reason I knew this was because my school cafeteria served fish sticks on Fridays.

I knew only one kid who wasn't either Protestant or Catholic. He was Jewish, which didn't make any difference to me. He and I were good friends, although I don't ever remember us talking about our respective religions and beliefs. Kids just didn't do things like that in those days. As for the other religions in other parts of the world, my family simply lumped them together in one category labeled "heathens" or "pagans." The sum total of my knowledge of these people was gathered from the slide shows the missionaries brought to our church when they were on furlough. That world seemed far removed from my cozy and safe environment. The closest I got to it personally was when my mom put some of my old clothes in the missionary barrel and when we prayed at the dinner table for all the missionaries serving in foreign fields.

We're Not in Kansas Anymore

I don't know when the shift away from this little world of Protestants and Catholics took place, but I finally noticed it when my wife and I returned to California from Texas (where it was all about Baptists and non-Baptists, as I mentioned in chapter 8). By that time we had two kids, and before long they were in school. That's when I noticed that the religious scene had shifted. No longer was it a two-tier system; it was multitiered. In addition to Protestants and Catholics, some Hindus, Sikhs, Muslims, and Buddhists attended the schools and lived in our neighborhoods—and my kids made friends with all of them.

This new multiculturalism in our kids' school and our neighborhood reflected the larger trends taking place in our city—the same city where I grew up—and in cities across America. Because of new immigration trends and patterns, no longer were people landing in New York or Los Angeles and then staying there. They were fanning out across the land, bringing with them their customs and beliefs.

Along with this shift in demographics came a shift in the general attitude toward Christianity. In the old days, Christianity was revered along with America and apple pie. Maintaining that kind of reputation is easy when your rivals are in a foreign field somewhere. But when people with different ideas about God and faith move next door, the landscape changes in a profound way.

Blaming the liberals (especially the ACLU) for taking prayer out of schools, Christ out of the Christmas pageants, and the giant granite Ten Commandments slabs out of the courthouse plazas is way too easy and simplistic. The plain fact is that we no longer live in a culture dominated by one system of belief. "In God We Trust" may still be on our money, and the flag salute may still contain the phrase "One nation under God," but people with different ideas about God live here and have every right under our constitution to practice their beliefs without being forced to embrace what many people thought was (or would become) the official religion of America.

Sadly, many Christians are upset that competing ideologies and religious beliefs have been given an equal platform in our culture. But people with competing beliefs and ideologies are here, and they deserve to be treated the way those of us who grew up in a mono-religious culture were treated—with respect.

In the old days, Christianity was revered along with America and apple pie. Maintaining that kind of reputation is easy when your rivals are in a foreign field.

The Postmodern Shift

Another aspect of our multicultural world is hitting people kind of hard. These days many people see Christianity as the odd man out. The king isn't exactly dead, but lots of people think Christianity is the big bully who needs to be taken down a notch—or more. Young people today aren't just making friends with kids of other faiths, the way my children did. They are interested in their ideas and beliefs, and they don't like hearing Christians condemn them as wrong.

We simply can't blame postmodernism and its introduction of "relative truth" into our vocabulary for this new shift in thinking. Many young people today—indeed, many people of all ages—believe that spiritual truth is everywhere and in every religion. The view that Christianity alone contains all truth for all people appears intolerant and judgmental.

We have seen this shift firsthand in the responses we get from the readers of our books. In case you haven't yet been to our website (hint, hint), I will tell you that we have written a whole bunch of books about God and Christianity, and in every one of them we invite our readers to send us e-mails with their comments and questions. When we first started writing books, the questions Bruce and I received were primarily doctrinal. People wanted to know about the Trinity, they were concerned about whether they were saved, and they were interested in the proofs for the existence of God.

More recently, we have seen a shift in the kinds of questions we receive. These days we don't get as many doctrinal questions. More typically, our e-mail box fills up with questions about morality.

- Does the Bible really say that homosexuality is wrong?

- Does God object to premarital sex?

- I had an abortion last year. Does God hate me?

- My brother was a Christian, but he committed suicide. Is he going to hell?

The questions aren't that succinct. They are usually connected to real-life stories from real people, and believe me, their questions sometimes tear our hearts out. On top of that, the questions are tough to answer. Sometimes the best response is to say that God really does care despite outward circumstances.

We have also noticed that the questions we receive from the people who read our books—and this goes to the heart of this chapter—have to do with certain beliefs about God and His nature. People aren't looking for information about God as much as they are looking for an explanation. Because of the infusion of different beliefs about God into our culture and because many people today have not studied the Bible, they are increasingly questioning things about God and salvation that people accepted without question in the past. Here are some real-life samples of the kinds of questions we receive:

- My question has to do with people who have never heard of Jesus. Is it true that you have to accept Jesus as Lord and Savior in order to go to heaven? If so, what about people who have never heard of Jesus? Even if they somehow know there is a Supreme Being, what good does that do if they don't know the "plan of salvation"?

- What happened to the people who lived before Jesus was sent down to save us? How could they have a chance to go to heaven if they didn't know about Jesus?

- If you believe that a person needs to believe in Jesus in order to be saved, where does that leave Jewish people who don't believe Jesus is the Messiah? Will they be saved, or will they be banished to hell? What about Muslims, who believe in God but not Jesus?

- It is difficult to fathom that all non-Christians will go to hell. Is that what the Bible really says?

- Is it okay for a Christian to study other religions? I don't understand the other religions and would like to learn more about them, but I'm not sure if it's okay with God, because I know he is a jealous God. I'm worried that if I study other religions, God will consider it blasphemy against him.

As I look at those questions, I don't see people who are out of line or angry. The people who write and tell us that they want nothing to do with a God who allows suffering and evil aren't antagonistic. The people who are frustrated because they think God hates gays aren't agnostic. The people who doubt God's existence aren't atheists. All of these people have something in common: They are looking for something meaningful to hang on to. They don't like the God who is, so they substitute a God they want. But is that the unforgivable sin? In my view, nobody is qualified to reshape God into his or her image, but that doesn't disqualify people spiritually speaking. God still loves them. God still cares about them.

Yet some Christians take these doubts and questions about God personally, and their first inclination is to fight back. They think that anyone who questions God is assaulting the truth. So they label these doubters as angry, antagonistic, agnostic, and atheistic. Even worse, they view people with doubts and competing ideas as the opposition, the enemy. So they are ready and willing to fight back. These are the kinds of Christians I can't stand.

I Can't Stand Christians Who Think They Have a Monopoly on Truth

Plenty of ordinary Christians feel as if their faith and way of life are being assaulted by the media, by members of the academic elite, and by people who follow other religions and cults. Some Christians may come to this conclusion on their own. But I believe most of them think this way because some influential and very vocal Christian leaders are working Christians into a frenzy. If you read the books and listen to the tirades of these leaders, you would think that Christians in America are under siege from the powers of darkness. They would have you believe that we are at war for the soul of our nation and the church, and unless Christians position themselves for battle, all will be lost.

These leaders don't pay attention to reasonable, thoughtful, and godly people like John Stott, who believes that the greatest threat to the Christian church is not from without but from within. They don't heed the words of the apostle Paul, who criticized the Galatians—calling them foolish at one point—for falling for some crazy ideas fed to them by a few overly zealous Christians.

That's exactly what's happening today. Many Christians are following the advice of the extremists who want to make enemies of people who desperately need Jesus. Yes, the Christopher Hitchenses of the world are saying some pretty nasty things about God and Christians, but so what? Should we be surprised that the world hates the followers of Jesus? Isn't that what Jesus told us would happen? We think we have it bad, but Jesus' enemies put him to death. Rather than lashing out, he asked his Father to forgive them because they didn't know what they were doing. Not us. We're not into forgiveness. We want revenge.

An Incredible Opportunity

Without question, a lot of bad ideas out there fly in the face of Christianity. Many belief systems are, quite frankly, pretty goofy. But rather than taking this personally and feeling threatened by competing beliefs, we need to recognize the incredible opportunity we have to share the good news about Jesus Christ—the *true* truth as Francis Schaeffer called it—with people who are searching for meaning.

We may wish that the people living in our neighborhoods, serving on the city council, and teaching in our schools didn't picture God as...

- an impersonal force that infuses every part of the universe, or
- a spirit that inhabits every person like a kind of divine light, or
- a powerful creator who made the universe and then took a long vacation, never to return, or
- something that doesn't exist at all.

They may have the wrong idea about God, but at least they're thinking about him! We may not like what they're saying about God, but at least he's in the conversation. They may not believe in the God of the Bible, but at least they want to believe in *something*. And here's something else to think about. Buried somewhere beneath their questions about God and their doubts about him are some very personal questions:

- Why am I here?
- How did I get here?
- How do I fit into this world?
- When my life is over, where am I going?

We've all faced these "meaning of life" questions at one time or another. If you have found the answers to your questions in a personal, loving God, then guess what—you have the answers that can help others who are still searching. Why in the world would any of us who have found the true truth choose to fight the people who are asking questions like these when we could instead be talking about Jesus and demonstrating his love?

> Rather than feeling threatened by competing belief systems, we need to recognize the incredible opportunity we have to share the good news about Jesus Christ.

What Does God Think About All of This?

I think God wants us to meet the challenges of the various philosophies and worldviews that are at our doorstep, and he seems to be orchestrating things in the world so that his message can go out in greater and more effective ways. The Scriptures tell us that God directs the hearts of kings and nations (Proverbs 21:1; Acts 17:26-27). Might he have brought about the migration of people and their cultures across seas and over continents so that we can share the gospel with them at this particular time in history? I think so. And let's not get so self-focused that we think it's all about America. God is doing his work in mighty ways around the world in places where America has little or no influence.

In his landmark book *The Next Christendom,* noted scholar Philip Jenkins reports that for the last 500 years, the story of Christianity has been tied to Europe and North America. Not any more. "Over the past century," he writes, "the center of gravity in the Christian world has shifted inexorably southward, to Africa, Asia, and Latin America. Already today, the largest Christian communities on the planet are to be found in Africa and Latin America."[1]

And these new communities are not necessarily Presbyterian or Baptist (sorry, Texas). More than likely they are Pentecostal. Jenkins says that current trends indicate the number of Pentecostal believers is on track to reach one billion worldwide by 2050. "In terms of the global religions, there will by that point be roughly as many Pentecostals as Hindus, and twice as many as there are Buddhists."[2] (Hey, we better get used to the idea that God doesn't work through Baptists and Presbyterians alone.)

So while the pundits and doomsayers are wringing their hands, God is on the move around the globe. I can think of at least four reasons why this is happening.

First, God loves the world. In fact, he loves it so much that he sent his only Son to earth to die for all of humanity so that anyone who believes in him will have eternal life (John 3:16). Contrary to what people may tell you, Jesus didn't come to condemn the world but to rescue it (John 3:17). God's new work in the world is part of his rescue plan.

Second, God doesn't want people to die in their sins, so he is giving everyone more time to turn to him. I think God keeps pushing back the time of Christ's return (like our editors do for us when we write a book). God hasn't lost track of time. He is being patient for our sake (2 Peter 3:9). Still, a time will come when God will bring down the hammer, so to speak, and it could happen any time (2 Peter 3:10). So we better not sit around worrying about the future. We need to get with God's plan now.

Third, God is not bothered by those who question and doubt him. Read how patiently God answered Moses when he doubted that God could use someone like him to rescue the Israelites from slavery (Exodus 3:1-22). Read how Jesus met at night with Nicodemus, a Jewish religious leader, in order to answer his questions and satisfy his doubts (John 3:1-21). Read how Jesus, following his resurrection, didn't condemn one of his followers who doubted that Jesus was risen, but instead tenderly gave him the proof he was seeking (John 20:26-29).

Finally, God will give us the ability to relate to people of other cultures and other faiths. I'm not saying we shouldn't prepare ourselves by learning what others believe (more about that in a minute). But sometimes when we know what to say, we don't say it—or when we know what to do, we don't do it—because we are afraid we aren't good enough. It's not our job to be good enough. Our job is to be obedient and do what God is asking. When the small group of believers began preaching the gospel in Jerusalem to a multicultural throng right after Jesus had returned to heaven, God "translated" their words so that everyone could understand them in their own language (Acts 2:1-13). If we simply step out and speak the truth in love to our neighbors—whether they are Hindus, Buddhists, Muslims, or outright skeptics—God will translate the message of our words and deeds so that their hearts will hear them.

Try This Approach

Do you think it's time for a new approach? I certainly do. The old way of seeing the people who oppose Christianity as our enemies is not the way of Christ. Besides, he told us to love our enemies and to pray for those who persecute us (Matthew 5:43-44). Yes, some bad things are going on in the world, but that doesn't mean we should circle the wagons into a tight Christian subculture, get on the defensive, and fight back. We need to do what Paul said: "Be careful how you live. Don't live like fools, but like those who are wise. Make the most of every opportunity in these evil days" (Ephesians 5:15-16).

When we Christians relate to people of other faiths (or no faith at all), here's what we need to do in order to make the most of every opportunity.

Find Out What We Have in Common

This goes to the heart of what this chapter is all about. Some Christians think they have a monopoly on truth, which by implication means that other belief systems can't possibly be true. Now, I certainly don't agree with the common perception in the culture that all religions basically contain the same truth presented in different ways. According to this view, God lives at the top of a very big mountain, and all the religions and belief systems in the world are like different trails that make their way to the top. Just as every trail eventually reaches the summit, every religion eventually reaches God.

Here's the problem with this thinking: All religions can't be true because all religions are different and mutually exclusive at various points, especially as you climb higher on the mountain. For example, Christians and Muslims both believe in one God. But as we compare the characteristics of the God of Islam (Allah) with the characteristics of the God of the Bible (Jehovah), we soon find clear distinctions. But we can agree on the single truth that there is one God. Just because a

Muslim believes that doesn't make it false. It's still a true statement. Like-wise, Hindus have assigned the Christlike qualities of love and grace to Vishnu. This god is not Christ, but does that nullify the truth that love and grace are eternal qualities? Of course not.

So even though I would disagree that all religions contain the *same* truth, I can confidently say that every religion contains *some* truth. That's why I like to say, There is truth in everything, but not everything is true.

When relating to our Hindu, Muslim, Buddhist, Jewish, and Mormon neighbors, we need to find the truth we have in common and use that as a platform to share Christ, showing them love and respect.

Paul and the Athenians

Paul gave us a terrific example of how to engage people of other faiths with the true gospel of Christ. In the book of Acts you can read about an encounter Paul had with some citizens of Athens, a city filled with temples, idols, and altars to the various gods and goddesses of mythology. Paul was walking through the city when he noticed a particular idol marked with the inscription, "To an Unknown God." Paul used this to engage some Greek philosophers. He made three points (you can read the complete story in Acts 17:16-34):

Introduction: the unknown God. Paul complimented the philosophers for being "very religious." He isn't saying that they are already following the one true God without knowing his name. He is merely setting up the question everyone needs to ask and answer: Who is God?

Main point: the one true God. Paul succinctly described the one true God by pointing to his attributes and acts of creation. God is the source of life and breath, and he is personally involved with his created beings.

Conclusion: turn to God. Though he did not mention Jesus by name, Paul clearly concluded his portion of the debate with the message of Christ. He told the philosophers to "repent of their sins and turn to him."

Paul didn't criticize or condemn the philosophers in a city full of idols. He found the truth he had in common with them (he even quoted their own poets) and used that as a platform to share Christ.

Know the Differences

Although Christianity shares some common truth with other religions, some of the differences are significant, and identifying them is important. My friend Craig Hazen, who is an expert in comparative religions, recommends that anyone who wants to do a serious study of the great world religions should study Christianity first. "It's the only religion that's testable," he says. "So you need to start with Christianity and measure all of the other religions against it rather than the other way around."

Some people take offense to this approach because they think Christians are once again setting themselves up as superior. Other people think this is an absurd approach because in their view, religion is subjective. They think it's merely a personal experience and a matter of individual preference. I agree that belief is intensely personal and filled with experience, but that doesn't exclude the possibility that one religion can be more solidly grounded in reality than another. I certainly believe that about Christianity for two reasons.

First, Christianity is true in what it says about God. All religious belief systems talk about God and the supernatural questions in one way or another. But Christianity presents God as he really is: the self-existent, eternal, personal Creator God who has revealed himself to humankind through the world he created (this is called "general revelation") and through the person of Jesus Christ (known as "special revelation").

Second, Christianity is true to the way things really are. What I mean by this is that Christianity gives reasonable explanations for the way things are in the natural world. For one thing, the truths of Christianity are consistent with history. The Bible is filled with facts about real people and real events in real time in ways that can be verified. For another, the truths of Christianity are consistent with what we know about the natural world. The Bible is not a scientific book, but its explanations for how the universe got here and how it operates are compatible with what science tells us is true. Finally, the truths of Christianity are consistent with reason. This means that rational beings can objectively evaluate the Christian belief system and find that it is reasonable and noncontradictory in its approach to the human condition. I'm not suggesting that Christianity is based entirely on reason, but I am saying that it's reasonable. It may go against common sense in some places, but it is never illogical.

Dr. Hazen suggests one additional characteristic of Christianity that sets it apart from other religions, and I think this one is pretty important: Christianity has Jesus at the center. Almost every religion includes Jesus in some way. For example, Muslims consider him a great prophet (they even say he was sinless). But only the belief system of Christianity is built around the person of Christ and what he did for humanity. As C.S. Lewis famously said, Jesus didn't leave us the option to treat him as just a prophet or a wise man. Jesus claimed to be the Messiah, the Son of God sent to earth to redeem the human race, alienated from God because of sin. His followers recognized this when he walked the earth (see Matthew 16:15-16). And his followers continue to acknowledge this today.

Show and Tell

This heading actually comes from the final chapter in Mike Erre's book *The Jesus of Suburbia*. It's not a new idea, but it hit me square between the eyes when I finally understood it. Christians are usually pretty good about telling people what they believe to be true. This isn't a bad thing.

If you know something that's been a great benefit to you and you know that it will benefit other people, you naturally want to tell them about it. My wife and I do with this with our kids all the time. We love them, so we give them advice on all kinds of things that we think will benefit them (of course, giving advice doesn't guarantee that advice will be taken). On the flipside, when we see our kids going in the wrong direction, we feel compelled to straighten them out.

Now, we can give advice and make corrections in two ways. The first is to tell people what we think. For parents, this falls under the category of "do as I say," and sometimes this is necessary. The other way is to show people what we think by the way we live our lives. For parents, this falls under the category of "do as I do." Why do parents sometimes say to their children, "Do as I say, not as I do"? Because telling people is a whole lot easier than showing them. But that doesn't mean telling is better than showing.

> Preach the gospel at all times and
> when necessary use words.
>
> St. Francis of Assisi

When we "share our faith," we need both means of communication. Unless our telling is reinforced by our showing, the telling will often fall on deaf ears. And if our showing contradicts what we are telling people, we will destroy the very message we are trying to communicate. We have all seen how damaging this kind of hypocrisy can be (and we don't have to look to our public figures for examples—we are all guilty of this). On the other hand, we have also seen how a simple act of showing can speak louder than any words.

One of the best examples of this is found in the Bible. John tells the story of a blind man whom Jesus healed (John 9:1-34). Even though Jesus performed a miracle, the religious leaders were upset because he had healed the man on the Sabbath, which was a violation of their regulations. The leaders questioned the man and demanded, "What's your opinion about this man who healed you?" The man did his best to offer an explanation, but it didn't satisfy the leadership. They pressed him further, asking, "But what did he do...How did he heal you?" What they really wanted the man to admit was that Jesus was a sinner because he had healed on the Sabbath.

The former blind man was through telling because that clearly wasn't working, so he responded in the only way he knew. "I don't know whether he is a sinner," the man replied. "But I know this: I was blind, and now I can see!"

What a lesson for those of us who think we can persuade people by trying to convince them that we have the truth and they don't, that we are right and they are wrong. When it's all said and done, the greatest demonstration of the truth and power of God is in our lives, not our words.

I'm Fine with God...

but I Can't Stand Christians Who Give Christ a Bad Name

I was on a plane last week, and I experienced that rare joy of having a vacant seat next to me. I was thrilled at the prospect of luxuriating in this unexpected tranquility...until the plane lifted off the runway. Across the aisle was a young father and his very much younger son. The kid was about four years old. It was the kid's first plane trip; I know that because he shouted it to all the passengers. I'm sure even the pilot heard the kid's screechy voice through the steel-reinforced, terrorist-proof, vault-like cockpit door. The vociferous child squealed with delight at every new sight he spied—sky, clouds, tiny people, little cars, an M&M (not outside, but one he found on the floor). Because I used to be a kid myself, I'm as sensitive as the next person to a child's enchantment. But the incessant shrieking was pushing me to the breaking point and challenging my Christianity. Didn't this kid ever learn about using an "inside voice"?

I felt like a jerk because I was getting so mad at a little kid who was just exhibiting unrestrained enthusiasm. Ordinarily, I freely share my jerkousity with everyone around me. But on this day I was uncommonly restrained. I suspected that the mannish looking woman in seat 2B was really an undercover air marshall dressed incognito and that she'd arrest me if I confronted the kid and threatened to stuff his Kermit plush toy down his tiny trachea. So I sat and stewed and tried to think of a loophole to my dilemma.

Then it occurred to me. I was mad at the kid, but I couldn't take any action because of societal proprieties. (And I really didn't want to be a bully anyway.) But I should really have been mad at the dad, and I wouldn't suffer any cultural ignominy for that. This wasn't a stretch of logic born out of desperation. It really was the dad's fault. How could he raise such a wild child? Why didn't he shush the kid? Why didn't he come equipped with codeine-enhanced cough syrup to help the kid sleep through the flight?

My resentment had been misplaced. I had too quickly picked the wrong target of my hostility. My originally perceived nemesis was blameless all along. I needed to redirect my anger (but I would choose to do so when the passenger in 2B went to the lavatory).

Similarly, the premise of this concluding chapter is that many people in our culture have mistakenly picked the wrong target for their anger. They are hostile toward Christ, but he is not their nemesis. Instead, just as I realized my problem was with the deadhead dad on my flight, people who are annoyed by Christianity should refocus their exasperation on the real underlying culprits—the kinds of Christians we have met in the preceding chapters.

Does a Christian by Another Name Still Smell the Same?

Extremist and clueless Christians have given Christianity a bad reputation in our culture. Most Christians realize that the demotion in our social standing is well deserved (and the ones who don't realize it are probably responsible for a good deal of the damage to our identity). The situation is so bad that we Christians are taking drastic and creative measures to abandon some of the baggage of our formerly revered terminology.

Next time you drive by Calvary Church, look closely at the sign. You'll see the faded outline from where the members pried off the letters because until a week ago their church was known as Calvary *Baptist*

Church. They aren't ashamed of their Baptist heritage; they are still part of the denomination. They just don't want to scare off visitors.

It goes beyond denominations. Christians aren't even admitting to being Christians. Now we prefer to refer to ourselves as "Christ followers." I'm not keen on this descriptive sleight of tongue. We know what "Christ follower" means, but to a non-Christian, it sounds as if Jesus is a drum major at the front of a parade and we're marching behind him in the band. Unfortunately, that only confirms the perception that we're nerds because everyone remembers that back in high school the kids who couldn't make it in sports ended up joining the marching band. (I know this because I was in the band.)

If you are really strong in your faith, your designation can be upgraded from "Christ follower." But we no longer use terms like "committed Christian" or "evangelical Christian." In an effort to avoid the stigma of the Christian label, we now go for the subtler "fully devoted follower of Christ." This just means you're still in the band but you're hoping to try out for the flag drill team.

It has gotten so bad that some people no longer admit to working for a Christian church or ministry. Now we just say we work for a "faith-based business." And there you have it. We have achieved the ultimate degree of obfuscation that we need. No one knows what "faith-based business" means. In today's shaky economy, every commercial enterprise is a faith-based business.

It is not as easy, however, for Jesus Christ to change his name. It's plastered throughout every Bible. If we Christians are truly interested in restoring the good name of Christ, we are going to have to do something more than tinker with our monikers.

They'd Laugh with Us If We Could Learn to Laugh at Ourselves

I'm fine with God. As we Christians view it, he is the perfect gentleman, and he doesn't force himself on us. The Bible lays out the meta-narrative of God's plan for humanity, and Christ provided us with a visible image of God himself. With all of that on the table, God leaves it up to us to decide what we are going to do with that information.

Some Christians, on the other hand, aren't as gracious as God. They understand the concept of free will, but they don't want us using it unless we freely exercise it as they think is best for us. These somewhat obstinate Christians are so intent on making everyone agree with them that they appear uptight much of the time.

Often these reactionary Christians are so intent on winning an argument about their faith that they forget to arm themselves with a sense of humor. Consider the fish stickers on some Christians' cars, for example. These Christians take great pride in that emblazoned symbol of their religious affiliation. But then the atheists, equally sincere and committed to their own beliefs, came out with a Darwin fish with little feet. Very clever. Unfortunately, many Christians couldn't laugh at the Darwin fish and couldn't leave it alone. Nope. They had to design a bigger Christian fish that was eating the Darwin fish with feet.

Ha! they thought. This will prove to everyone that Christianity is real. But wait—the bigger fish eating the smaller Darwin fish...doesn't that illustrate survival of the fittest? That's Darwinism! The Christians who were caught up in winning the fish sign wars are using a design that illustrates the principle of evolution.

Wouldn't they give a better impression of Christ if they could just learn to laugh at themselves?

Never Miss a Chance to Make a Buck

I don't mind actors and athletes trying to cash in on their celebrity status, but it is unseemly when Christian leaders do it. When they try to hawk stuff, the unspoken implication is that God wants you to buy it. Invoking God as a way to put leverage or guilt on a parishioner for a minister's own self-enrichment just seems unfair.

I don't mind that Jared Fogle is the spokesperson for Subway. But why was 76-year-old millionaire televangelist Pat Robertson shilling an "age-defying" diet shake for $21.99 (plus shipping)? Here is how the promo piece read on the Christian Broadcasting Network website:

> Did you know that Pat Robertson, through rigorous training, leg-pressed 2,000 pounds? How does he do it? Where does Pat find the time and energy to host a daily, national TV show, head a world-wide ministry, develop visionary scholars, while traveling the globe as a statesman?
>
> One of Pat's secrets to keeping his energy high and his vitality soaring is his age-defying protein shake. Pat developed a delicious, refreshing shake, filled with energy-producing nutrients. Discover what kinds of natural ingredients make up Pat's protein shake by registering for your FREE booklet today![1]

Christ drove the money changers out of the temple, but actions such as Robertson's seem to show that Christians are doing a little money changing of their own. Why does a guy who sold his media network for $1.9 billion need to sell protein shakes at $21.99 a pop? And does he have to use apparent exaggerations about his 2000-pound leg-press accomplishment to hype his sales? (I say "apparent" only because the all-time record for the leg press at Florida State University was set by Dan Kendra at a paltry 1355 lbs, which would make 76-year-old Robertson a record holder of some sort).[2] And what about truth in advertising? Come on, "age-defying"? Really? Have you seen Pat Robertson? Oh sure, he is fit and handsome for a man of 76 years, but those 76 years have not been defied.

When Christians try to pull off antics such as this, they give Christ a bad name because they do it under his banner.

Trying Too Hard to Be Cool Is Really Uncool
Christians are trying so hard to be cool in the eyes of the world that we come across as desperate. And nothing could be more uncool than that.

God offers us the answer to life. He shows where humanity went wrong, he shows us how to get back on track, and he asks us to trust him. We Christians think, *I believe it, but nobody else will.* So we have to make ourselves look appealing to the culture. And that's hard to do because we aren't allowed to do the fun stuff. So we think that somehow we've got to show the culture we're cool in order to attract them to our theology.

Accordingly, we set about to promote Christianity with secular marketing techniques. But we don't give them the same degree of creativity our secular counterparts use, so our attempts come across as lame. We copy a famous marketing slogan and just slip Jesus into it. In what is probably illegal trademark infringement against Coca-Cola, we wear T-shirts with the Coke style and font that say, "Things go better with Christ." I'm sure the Milk Advisory Board isn't crazy about our ripping off their slogan for our "Got Christ?" campaign. And church marquees are a tragic public display of our lack of creativity: "Don't just have a good day, have a God day."

We'll even compromise our doctrine for the sake of a slogan that makes us appear hip (or so we think). Even though the story of the gospel is pretty creative and can stand on its own, we think we can do better at grabbing someone's attention. But in our attempt to be clever, we play fast and loose with our doctrine. (We don't want anyone else messing with our doctrine, but we can make some concessions with it for the sake of marketing.)

Remember the highway billboard campaign concocted by some Christian marketing genius? It was designed to shock drivers with the reality and presence of God, as if God had written the messages. One billboard said this:

> "Don't make me come down there." —God

But isn't that the entire message of the gospel—that God already actually came down to earth? Isn't that exactly what Christians are trying to convince people about? I'm sure God wants to slap that billboard copywriter alongside the head and say, "I did come down already. Is that such a bad thing?"

These Christians have people thinking that Christ is a lame and desperate marketer. And if you have to work that hard to sell what you've got, suddenly what you've got doesn't appear to be that great.

False Advertising to Close the Salvation Sale

It goes without saying, but I'll say it anyway. Evangelical Christians believe they must evangelize. Some of them keep track of salvation tallies as if they were racking up points in a video game. In their effort to save souls, these well-meaning Christians tend to stretch the truth to close the sale. People in the real-estate industry call it "permissible puffing." In Christian circles, it is called "speaking evangelistically."

Usually, the offending misrepresentation takes the form of a material omission—we intentionally omit a crucial item that might otherwise change a person's decision. For example, we don't mention (or at least don't emphasize) that the Christian life has a lot of struggles.

Maybe that's why very few churches have Bibles in the pew racks anymore. Plenty of space is available in those racks (because most churches have discarded their hymnals). But if we get a visitor coming to one of our services, we don't want a curious one to leaf through the Bible and find a verse like Luke 9:23 (KJV), where Jesus said, "If any man will come after me, let him deny himself, and take up his cross daily, and follow me." We don't want people finding out about this "take up his cross daily" business until after they have said the sinner's prayer. Oh, we won't lie to them if they ask about it, but we sure don't put that verse in our church's welcome brochure.

And we certainly don't tell anyone—visitors or our own Christian friends—if we are personally going through struggles in our spiritual

journey. This is perhaps the most worst-kept secret of the Christian life—
that God doesn't spare us from tough times. However, we pretend they
don't exist. We'll put the words of Jesus from John 10:10 (KJV) up on the
PowerPoint at church: "I am come that they might have life, and that
they might have it more abundantly." We do our best to sell a brand
of Christianity that comes complete with the abundant life. And it does,
but we aren't honest enough when talking with our Christian friends or
a salvation prospect to admit that the Christianity thing doesn't always
seem to be working for us. However, considering all that Christ has
done for us, the least we can do for him is to fake it.

Other times, the "evangelistically speaking" misrepresentation is a
blatant misstatement of fact. (Plain speak: a lie.) For example, I was
intrigued by an ad for a church in the religion section of my local
newspaper. In an unabashed attempt to suck in visitors, the ad said
that this was "the kind of church you've always wanted." That was a
promise I had to check out. Not surprisingly, the statement wasn't true.
They took an offering.

People must wonder about Christ if he is allowing us to parade around
in his name making misrepresentations for the sake of increasing the
membership of Club Christianity.

Why the Hostility?

Here's what troubles me as much as anything: Why do we Christians
feel compelled to be so hostile toward the rest of society? Why do we
have to come across in every cultural encounter as if we have the rod
of Moses and intend to beat people over the head with it?

I only have to pick up a daily newspaper to find an example. And
that's what I did while writing this chapter. My Christian brethren didn't
let me down. In the news was a story about a pastor from Southern
California who used church stationery to endorse a presidential
candidate. (I'll let you guess the political party.) This action could be
interpreted as improper campaigning by a charitable organization,

and the Washington-based Americans United for Separation of Church and State made an official request for the IRS to investigate the tax-exempt status of the pastor's church.

When faced with the prospect of an extensive and public IRS examination, the pastor did what any good Christian would do: He prayed. But his prayer wasn't for God's forgiveness or mercy on him and his church, and his prayer wasn't for guidance in negotiating with the IRS. His prayer wasn't even for strength to endure the process. Nope. Instead, his prayer was for God to bring misfortune into the lives of the members of Americans United for Separation of Church and State.[3]

The pastor showed his congregation Psalm 109 as a format for their prayers.

> Hold not thy peace, O God of my praise;
> For the mouth of the wicked and the mouth of the deceitful are opened against me: they have spoken against me with a lying tongue...
> Set thou a wicked man over him: and let Satan stand at his right hand...
> Let his days be few; and let another take his office.
> Let his children be fatherless, and his wife a widow.
> Let his children be continually vagabonds, and beg: let them seek their bread also out of their desolate places.
> Let the extortioner catch all that he hath; and let the strangers spoil his labor.
> Let there be none to extend mercy unto him: neither let there be any to favor his fatherless children.
> Let his posterity be cut off; and in the generation following let their name be blotted out...
> Let this be the reward of mine adversaries from the LORD, and of them that speak evil against my soul (Psalm 109:1-20 KJV).

Where's the "love your enemies" that Christ talked so much about? No wonder we Christians give Christ a bad name when we are guilty of conduct Christ himself would have condemned.

> Some Christians find fault as if a
> reward is being offered for it.

What Does God Think About All of This?

In his book *The Company of the Committed*, author Elton Trueblood said, "The test of the vitality of a religion is to be seen in its effect upon the culture."[4] If this statement is true, and I believe that it is, Christianity was once vital, but the contemporary version of Christianity is impotent. What's the difference between then and now? Not Christ. He didn't change. His principles of "love one another" and "love your enemies" have been the same. The precepts he taught in the Sermon on the Mount have stayed the same. The one component of Christianity that has changed are the Christians themselves. Or, I should say, we Christians ourselves.

We Christians of the current age owe it to Christ to repair the damage we have done to his public image. We are in a mode of crisis management, and modifications are necessary. All of the reconstructive work must take place in the hearts and minds of Jesus' followers so that our language and conduct are Christlike rather than discrediting to him.

Bringing Back the "Mental" to Fundamentalism

The word "fundamentalism" has a bad connotation. It suggests some wild-eyed radical who has lost touch with reality. It didn't always have such a bad implication, at least in the Christian context.

In chapter 8, Stan referred to the compilation of more than 100 essays by leading Christian scholars. This defense and survey of classical Christian thought was called *The Fundamentals*. And Christians who adhered to these doctrinal fundamentals became known as "fundamentalists."

In the recent decade, fundamentalists lost the character of being thoughtful and articulate. Instead, largely because of some of the issues we've highlighted in this book, they became known as lunatics. In other words, they lost the "mental" part of what they were all about.

If Christians are going to restore the perception of Christ as he is portrayed in the New Testament, we need to be more thoughtful about our faith. Instead of spending our time lashing out at the culture (which Christ never did), we should put our time to better use by trying to conform ourselves to Christ.

If Christians are going to project the correct image of Christ in our culture, we need to carefully choose our spokespersons and representatives. We should refuse to fall in line behind those Christian leaders who do not exhibit Christlike characteristics. This is why Stan and I are excited to be a part of ConversantLife.com, which presents credentialed Christian communicators who are thoughtful, articulate, and engaging in their discussion of the Christian faith and cultural issues. These communicators use humor and logic instead of wagging their fingers. While being true to the fundamentals of a faith rooted in Christ, we need to leave room for mystery about God and discussion with civility and honest doubt. The existence of Christ needs to be rediscovered in the creative arts and in the *professions* so he is not boxed into church buildings. We need to let Christ loose once again so he can be back on the streets with the people, letting people decide for themselves whether they want to follow him.

Making the Old Evangelism New Again

Some Christians are using the wrong brand of evangelism, trying to cram their faith down the throats of their unsuspecting victims. If this is the only form of evangelism Christians know, they should stop being so evangelistic. One thing is clear: This is not the brand of evangelism Christ had in mind when he encouraged his followers to be his witnesses.

The apostle Peter describes the ancient form of evangelism that Christians need to rediscover and employ: "If someone asks about your

Christian hope, always be ready to explain it. But do this in a gentle and respectful way" (1 Peter 3:15-16).

Christ-designed evangelism involves no finger pointing or throat cramming. Instead, Christ expects his followers to live an exemplary life that intrigues others (and doesn't repulse them). Notice that this verse implies that a discussion of personal faith will be initiated by someone else, not the Christian. Being prepared to give an answer supposes that someone is going to ask a question. That will only happen when Christians learn to attract people rather than repel them.

If I didn't know better, I'd believe that most of us Christians are carrying around Bibles that were misprinted and omitted 1 Peter 3:16—at least the part of the verse that says we are to respond to questions and engage in faith discussions with gentleness and respect. If we Christians took that approach, we could avoid or at least minimize all of the offensives we've identified in this book.

Christians don't need to revamp the culture in order to regain respect in society. We simply need to start conducting ourselves in the loving manner that Christ intended all along.

Notes

Chapter 1—I'm Fine with God...but I Can't Stand Christians Who Impose Their Morality on Others

1. James Warner, "Infallible Apologies," *SAIS Review*, vol. 25, no. 2, 67-68.

Chapter 2—I'm Fine with God...but I Can't Stand Christians Who Are Paranoid

1. Jim Taylor and Watts Wacker, *The 500-Year Delta: What Happens After What Comes Next* (New York, NY: Collins, 1998), 30.

2. Sam Harris, *Letter to a Christian Nation* (New York: Knoph, 2006), vii.

Chapter 3—I'm Fine with God...but I Can't Stand Christians Who Think They Are Correctly Right and Everyone Else Is Wrongly Left

1. Katha Pollitt, "Onward, Secular Soldiers," *The Nation*, September 24, 2007. Available online at www.thenation.com/doc/20070924/pollitt.

2. Gregory Boyd, *Myth of a Christian Nation* (Grand Rapids, MI: Zondervan, 2005), 70-71.

Chapter 4—I'm Fine with God...but I Can't Stand Christians Who Think Science Is the Enemy

1. John Morris, "Wrong on Two Counts," Institute for Creation Research. Available online at www.icr.org/article/3433/.

2. Wayne Grudem, *Systematic Theology* (Grand Rapids, MI: Zondervan, 1994), 196.

3. Much of the material in this section is taken from our book *Creation & Evolution 101* (Eugene, OR: Harvest House, 2001).

4. John Sailhamer, *Genesis Unbound* (Sisters, OR: Multnomah, 1996), 29.

5. Mike Erre, *The Jesus of Suburbia* (Nashville, TN: W Publishing, 2006), 171-72.

6. Bruce Bickel and Stan Jantz, *Bruce and Stan Search for the Meaning of Life* (Nashville, TN: W Publishing, 2001), 160.

7. Don Stoner, *A New Look At an Old Earth* (Eugene, OR: Harvest House, 1997), 33.

Chapter 5—I'm Fine with God...but I Can't Stand Christians Who Are Convinced God Wants Them Rich

1. See David van Biema and Jeff Chu, "Does God Want You to Be Rich?" *Time*, September 10, 2006.

2. See Jamie Dean, "Lone Sentry on the Wall," *World Magazine,* July 28, 2007.

3. See Dick Straub, "Superficiality and Christian Formation," *Culturewatch,* September 28, 2004.

4. See William Lobdell, "Pastor's Empire Built on Acts of Faith, and Cash," *Los Angeles Times,* September 19, 2004.

5. Lobdell, "Pastor's Empire Built on Acts of Faith, and Cash."

6. See William Lobdell, "TBN's Promise: Send Money and See Riches," *Los Angeles Times,* September 20, 2004.

7. Arlene Sanchez Walsh and Madison Trammel, "First Church of Prosperidad," *Christianity Today,* October 5, 2007.

8. Lobdell, "Pastor's Empire Built on Acts of Faith, and Cash."

9. John Avanzini, *Believers' Voice of Victory,* TBN broadcast, January 20, 1991.

10. Michael Okonkwo, *Controlling Wealth God's Way,* cited in Isaac Phiri and Joe Maxwell, "Gospel Riches," *Christianity Today,* October 5, 2007.

11. Paul Crouch, cited in Lobdell, "TBN's Promise: Send Money and See Riches."

12. Rick Warren, cited in Van Biema and Chu, "Does God Want You to Be Rich?"

Chapter 6—I'm Fine with God...but I Can't Stand Christians Who Fixate on the End of the World

1. Ronald Aronson, "The New Atheists," *The Nation.* Available online at www.thenation. com/doc/20070625/aronson.

2. Louis Sahagun, "'End Times' Religious Groups Want Apocalypse Soon," *Los Angeles Times,* June 22, 2006.

Chapter 7—I'm Fine with God...but I Can't Stand Christians Who Make Lousy Movies

1. Bruce Bickel and Stan Jantz, *Bruce and Stan Search for the Meaning of Life* (Nashville: W Publishing, 2001), 174.

2. Available online at www.sbcbaptistpress.org/bpnews.asp?ID=22495.

3. Bickel and Jantz, *Bruce and Stan Search for the Meaning of Life,* 176.

4. Cindy Crosby, "Left Behind: The Lawsuit," *Publishers Weekly,* February 26, 2001.

5. Bickel and Jantz, *Bruce and Stan Search for the Meaning of Life,* 175-176.

6. Bickel and Jantz, *Bruce and Stan Search for the Meaning of Life,* 175.

7. Bickel and Jantz, *Bruce and Stan Search for the Meaning of Life,* 42.

8. Bob Briner, *Roaring Lambs* (Grand Rapids: Zondervan, 1993), 40.

9. Michael Medved, "War Films, Hollywood, and Popular Culture," *Imprimis* (Hillsdale, MI: Hillsdale College, May 2005). Available online at www.hillsdale.edu/news/imprimis/archive/issue.asp?year=2005&month=05.

Chapter 8—I'm Fine with God...but I Can't Stand Christians Who Don't Know What They Believe

1. Mike Erre, *The Jesus of Suburbia* (Nashville, TN: W Publishing, 2006), xv.

2. Dan Kimball, *They Love Jesus but Not the Church* (Grand Rapids, MI: Zondervan, 2007), 189.

3. Michael J. Vlach, "Crisis in America's Churches: Bible Knowledge at All-Time Low," theologicalstudies.org. Available online at www.theologicalstudies.citymax.com/page/page/1573625.htm.

4. Erre, *The Jesus of Suburbia*, 155.

5. Erre, *The Jesus of Suburbia*, 171.

Chapter 9—I'm Fine with God...but I Can't Stand Christians Who Think They Have a Monopoly on Truth

1. Philip Jenkins, *The Next Christendom* (New York, NY: Oxford University Press, 2002), 2.

2. Jenkins, *The Next Christendom*, 8.

Chapter 10—I'm Fine with God...but I Can't Stand Christians Who Give Christ a Bad Name

1. www.cbn.com/communitypublic/shake.aspx.

2. Clay Travis, "ClayNation: Pat Robertson's Magical Protein Shake," *Spin on Sports*. Available online at cbs.sportsline.com/spin/story/9454343.

3. Connie King, "Prayer for Opponent's Misfortune Finds Little Support," *Los Angeles Times*, August 25, 2007, page B2.

4. Elton Trueblood, *The Company of the Committed: A Bold and Imaginative Re-Thinking of the Strategy of the Church in Contemporary Life* (New York: Harper Collins, 1979).

It's a Harsh,

Crazy,

Beautiful,

Messed Up,

Breathtaking

World...

And People Are Talking About It...

engage your faith